*U*NDERSTANDING AND SUPPORTING CHILDREN WITH ADHD

UNDERSTANDING AND SUPPORTING CHILDREN WITH ADHD

Strategies for Teachers, Parents and Other Professionals

Lesley Hughes and Paul Cooper

P·C·P

Paul Chapman
Publishing

Paul Chapman Publishing
A SAGE Publications Company
1 Oliver's Yard
55 City Road
London EC1Y 1SP

SAGE Publications Inc
2455 Teller Road
Thousand Oaks, California 91320

SAGE Publications India Pvt Ltd
B-42, Panchsheel Enclave
Post Box 4109
New Delhi 110 017

Library of Congress Control Number: 2006932948

A catalogue record for this book is available from the British Library

ISBN-978-1-4129-1860-2
ISBN-978-1-4129-1861-9 (pbk)

Typeset by Pantek Arts Ltd, Maidstone, Kent
Printed in Great Britain by Cromwell Press Ltd, Trowbridge, Wiltshire
Printed on paper from sustainable resources

CONTENTS

About the Authors   vi

How to use this book   vii

1   **Understanding ADHD**   1

2   **The ADHD Experience**   14

3   **ADHD and Medication: A Brief Consideration of the Evidence**   26

4   **ADHD and Schools**   30

5   **The Necessity of Collaborative Working**   44

6   **Models for Collaborative Working**   59

7   **Educational Interventions for ADHD**   70

8   **Food for Thought**   84

    Appendix: Diagnostic Criteria for Attention Deficit Hyperactive Disorder   91

    Glossary   93

    References   95

    Index   101

About the Authors

Dr. Lesley Hughes, PhD, MA, BSc, RGN, C.Psychol.
Faculty of Health and Social Care, University of Hull, UK

Lesley Hughes is a Chartered Psychologist (Research and Teaching) and Head of Inter-professional learning at the Faculty of Health and Social Care and the Hull York Medical School at the University of Hull. She is an active researcher in the field of interprofessional education and partnership working; including presenting the client's perspective on service provision and support. Lesley's research and experience of interprofessional education has resulted in her role as Executive Board Member for The Centre for Advancement in Inter-professional Education (CAIPE) www.caipe.org.uk and The International Association for Education and Collaborative Practice (InterEd) www.health-disciplines.ubc.ca/test3/index.php

Professor Paul Cooper, PhD, Med, MA, BA, DipEd, CPsychol, AFBPsS
School of Education, University of Leicester, UK

Paul Cooper, PhD is a Chartered Psychologist (Research and Teaching) and Professor of Education at the University of Leicester, where he is also Director of the Centre for Innovation in Raising Educational Achievement. He is an active researcher in the field of social, emotional and behavioural difficulties in schools and editor of the quarterly journal *Emotional and Behavioural Difficulties*.

Children with Attention Deficit Hyperactivity Disorder (ADHD) can be hard to include in a mainstream classroom, and managing their behaviour is often a challenge for parents and teachers. This book draws directly from real classroom and home experiences by exploring the reality of living with ADHD and identifies how effective management strategies can improve children's behaviour in and out of the classroom. The book adopts an inter-disciplinary approach, to provide teachers, special educational needs co-ordinators (SENCOs), newly qualified teachers, teaching assistants, learning mentors and student teachers working with children who have ADHD, with:

- strategies to deal with disruptive behaviours

- ways to channel children's positive characteristics

- advice on how teachers can support and guide parents

- behaviour management techniques to promote positive behaviour

- advice on collaborative working that will help teachers to build partnerships with other professionals.

The case studies incorporated into the text of this book are a composite of numerous children in various settings and are not specific to any one child, practitioner or setting; they are based on research undertaken for Lesley Hughes's PhD thesis at the University of Bradford. The names of all interviewees have been changed in order to respect the privacy of individuals involved.

The purpose of the research was to understand the reality of day-to-day living with ADHD, so that the knowledge and insight of individuals could inform the rhetoric theory that guides treatment and management programmes. Keeping in mind the recent government paper, *Every Child Matters* (DFES, 2003), which specifies, amongst other things, that whatever the child's background or their circumstances they are eligible to receive the support they need to be healthy, enjoy and achieve, and make a positive contribution, it is imperative therefore that children with ADHD have their needs understood, and met. However, considering the sensitivity of doing research with children, and especially children with behaviour and attention difficulties, an 'informant style' of interview was used to retrieve information: this is similar to the cognitive interview technique described by Roy (1991). The process, when related to the child's behaviour, encourages the child to recall any aspect of their behaviour occurring on that day. Reliability of the child's accounts came from obtaining reports from parents and teachers about the child's behaviour. Although the detail of the accounts will vary from that of the child's, the general observations of the event will be similar. In addition, the accounts from parents and teachers can be used to gain access to the child's deeper levels of thinking by allowing the researcher to use this information to encourage the child to elaborate on specific events occurring in the classroom or in the home.

The book draws on the authors' knowledge, and research experiences, to provide readers with insight not only about ADHD, but also about the lives of the children with the diagnosis, and the impact their home and school environment has on them and their behaviour. The authors take this information and provide readers with approaches and models that will enable them to rethink their approaches to managing and supporting children with ADHD.

Throughout the book there is an emphasis on the importance of collaborative working for achieving and maintaining support for children, and, where appropriate, examples from the research study explain how these models can be implemented in practice.

For ease of reading the terms in the glossary are in **bold** _when they first appear in the text._

Understanding ADHD

Attention Deficit Hyperactivity Disorder (**ADHD**) is a diagnosis of the American Psychiatric Association (APA, 1994) (see Appendix). It describes behavioural symptoms of **inattention**, **impulsiveness** and **hyperactivity** that are presented to a degree that significantly interferes with a person's family and peer relations as well as their educational and/or occupational functioning. This chapter focuses on:

◆ ADHD: its nature and origins
  - Inattentiveness
  - Impulsiveness
  - Hyperactivity
  - Correlates of ADHD
◆ The evolution of ADHD into an educational issue
  - Evidence base for ADHD: **cognitive** process
  - Evidence base for ADHD: **bio-psychosocial** construct
  - ADHD and cognitive ability
  - Assessment and diagnosis of ADHD
◆ What children, parents and teachers say about ADHD
  - Case studies
◆ Points to remember
◆ Key points to remember

ADHD: its nature and origins

There are, according to current diagnostic criteria, three types of ADHD seen in children, the:

■ hyperactive/impulsive type

■ inattentive type

■ combined hyperactive-impulsive/inattentive type.

Somewhere between 3 and 6 per cent of school-aged children and young people are affected by ADHD, a condition which crosses social and cultural boundaries but is more commonly seen in boys (Tannock, 1998). According to the **National Institute for Clinical Excellence** (NICE, 2000), in the UK this means that between 3 and 5 per cent of school-aged children have ADHD, making it one of the most commonly diagnosed childhood disorders. Although considered for many years a disorder restricted to childhood, it is now believed to be carried forward into adulthood by between 30 and 70 per cent of those who present the symptoms in childhood (Hinshaw, 1994; Weiss and Hechtman, 1993). The developmental course of ADHD usually begins between the ages of 3 and 4, though some children show evidence of the disorder in early infancy, and others not until the ages of 5 or 6 years (Anastopoulos, 1999).

Typically, children with the symptoms of ADHD present the following behavioural and attentional difficulties in classroom and other settings:

- a pattern of **behaviour** that distracts them and those around them

- difficulty sustaining attention on tasks and activities

- difficulty starting and completing tasks and activities

- appear to be inattentive to verbal instruction

- appear disorganized and forgetful

- appear to have an immature approach to activities.

In the following sections we look at the core areas of inattentiveness, hyperactivity and impulsiveness in more detail to understand how they impact on behaviour.

Inattentiveness

Children with ADHD exhibit apparent difficulties in sustaining attention when engaged in educational tasks and other activities. They will tend to have difficulty beginning new tasks, be easily distracted from most tasks once they have started, and have difficulty returning to a task after being distracted from it (Douglas, 1983). In the classroom, you may have found that children with ADHD are less inclined to focus on tasks that are repetitive or dull. However, you could try providing them with tasks that offer an element of novelty, and tasks that bring an immediate reward. They tend to want immediate rewards for their efforts in tasks, preferring short-term gains to long-term rewards (Campbell and Ewing, 1990), therefore when teachers offer varied tasks with immediate rewards this can help to focus the child's attention.

It is also suggested that for a task to promote sustained attention, the child needs to 'self-pace' or 'self-choose' rather than have a task selected or paced by others. This theory proposes that the 'choosing' of the task is in itself the intrinsic reward (Hinshaw,1994). It seems that in order for a child to pay attention to a task, an extrinsic reward may not be a sufficient form of motivation for children with ADHD. However, having an intrinsic interest in a task may be a motivator in itself. This observation has important consequences for behaviour management strategies that rely on the use of extrinsic rewards.

An alternative to the sustained attention hypothesis is proposed by Sergeant and Scholten (1985), who argue that the core problem for people with these kinds of difficulties lies in a deficit in motor output. They propose that children with ADHD experience severe problems in regulating their motor control and, as a consequence, are slow to perform tasks. Teachers may find that by giving children with ADHD extra time, they are able to complete tasks.

The differing views as to the nature of what appears to be 'inattentiveness' illustrate the complexity of the ADHD phenomenon. As will be shown later in this chapter, there are also differences in the **neurological** explanations that have been proposed in relation to ADHD. There may be good reasons why the apparently same surface behaviour could be the product of different neurological and cognitive influences. Chief amongst these is the influence of experiential and environmental factors. Wood (1988) argues that concentration is not a natural ability and that self-regulation has to be learned. This is in line with the thinking of seminal cognitive psychologist Lev Vygotsky (1962), who argued that many of a person's higher-level cognitive skills, for example reasoning, are highly dependent upon the kinds of experiences they have had of interaction with other people. This might be taken to suggest that attentional problems may sometimes be the product, in part at least, of insufficient exposure to situations in which the regulation of attention has been required and socially fostered.

Impulsiveness

Impulsive behaviour in children with ADHD is often displayed in the form of apparent impatience, as in blurting out answers in class when they have been instructed to 'raise your hand and wait to be called upon to answer'. Other examples include difficulty in waiting their turn in games or conversations. In the classroom, their restlessness may resemble that of a butterfly as they move quickly from one task to another. Those observing such impulsive behaviour may complain that the child has a careless and unfocused approach to classroom activities. Complaints may also be made about the child's rudeness, especially when he or she appears to act without thought for others, such as when he or she interrupts or intrudes into the activities of others. These children may appear to be antisocial, because the social norms adhered to by others do not seem to serve as a frame of reference for them.

However, tests to measure impulsiveness have been criticized. Sonuga-Barke et al. (1992) found that children's motivation and delay on a task were affected by the understanding of the test reward and concluded that it was the children's understanding that dictated whether they responded impulsively. Taylor (1995) argues that research into impulsive behaviour needs to consider the decision-making behind the behavioural response. A later study concludes that a negative experience of delay aversion will 'discourage children from gaining experience in situations where delay is involved and may therefore hold them back from learning the skills of inhibition' (Taylor, 1999: 614).

It is generally accepted that impulsiveness, like inattentiveness, is a failure of **self-regulation**. This means that individuals with impulse problems have difficulty in controlling a behavioural response to a given stimulus. The cognitive functions by which most of us manage to stop ourselves from giving in to an impulse (for example, to overspend on our credit card, or eat the whole box of chocolates) are either not activated, or are activated too slowly to be effective (Barkley, 1997).

Teachers might find that by providing children with clear instruction, and ensuring that they understand what is being asked of them (even if this means repeating the instructions), that they are better able to engage with the task and are therefore more focused.

Hyperactivity

Hyperactivity can be defined as commonly occurring, minor motor activities that are performed at abnormally high intensity and high frequency levels. These behaviours include: hand- and foot-tapping; bodily fidgeting; motor tics, talking, climbing and walking around. Typically, among school-aged children hyperactive behaviour is exhibited in the rapid movement of a child around the class when the situation calls for him or her to sit in his or her seat; excessive fidgeting when seated and/or excessive talking.

These behaviours are often interpreted as indications that the child is ignoring instructions. In addition, despite being told often, by parents and teachers, to correct their behaviour, these children show little evidence of improvement or of attempting to change. Again, normally effective strategies for social regulation seem to be ineffective with these children. Douglas (1983) questions whether hyperactivity is actually a symptom of the condition, suggesting that the core symptoms of inattention and impulsivity may mimic hyperactivity. Questions remain as to the relationship between attentional problems with hyperactivity and those which occur without obvious signs of hyperactivity. Are Attention Deficit Disorder (ADD) and Attention Deficit Hyperactivity Disorder (ADHD) simply different manifestations of the same underlying condition, or are they the product of different cognitive deficits? This question is dealt with in more detail later.

You may find that children displaying hyperactive behaviour benefit not only from clarity about how you want them to behave in a particular situation, or with a task, but also that this information is given and repeated slowly (Hughes, 2004). Such advice is not so that this type of management makes the child feel isolated as a special case, but that they recognize that you are helping them to manage themselves.

Correlates of ADHD

There are many seriously debilitating social, emotional, behavioural correlates of ADHD. Individuals with ADHD are more likely than the general population to experience social isolation, accidental injury and psychological disturbance (Tannock, 1998). People with undiagnosed ADHD are often dismissed as incompetent, disorganized, aggressive, disruptive, lazy, untrustworthy, neglectful, selfish, accident prone, antisocial and/or asocial. School students with ADHD are prone to poorer academic performance than their scores on standardized tests of cognitive ability predict (Barkley, 1990; Hinshaw, 1994). In the UK, Hayden (1997) found the symptoms of hyperactivity to be one of a range of predictors of formal exclusion from school among children of primary school age.

It is probably the case that children with ADHD have a high likelihood of finding themselves in special schools for children with Social, Emotional and Behavioural Difficulties (SEBD), or other specialist provision. One study of 85 children aged 6 to 13 (including only three girls) attending a special school for children with SEBD in the UK, found a prevalence rate for ADD (APA, 1980) of 70 per cent. The children were assessed using a standardized screening questionnaire completed by teachers, and a psychiatric interview with parents (Place et al., 2000). An earlier study by Vivian (1994), of children in a similar setting, found the prevalence of hyperkinesis (that is, extreme hyperactivity forming a subset of ADHD [NICE, 2000]) to be 40 per cent.

Other studies have found the symptoms of ADHD to be associated with serious relationship problems, marital breakdown, employment difficulties (Hinshaw, 1994) and imprisonment (Farrington, 1990; Weiss and Hechtman, 1993). In addition to these problems ADHD is found to co-occur with a wide range of other difficulties at rates of between 25 and 60 per cent, including Specific Learning Difficulties (SpLD/dyslexia), Conduct Disorder (CD), Oppositional Defiant Disorder (ODD), Depression (DD) and Anxiety Disorder (AD) (Angold et al.,1999; Barkley et al.,1990).

The emotional and behavioural 'co-morbid' disorders (CD, ODD, DD, AD) tend to emerge during the adolescent years, giving rise to the hypothesis that these are socially induced problems that occur as a result of the misunderstanding and mismanagement of the primary ADHD symptoms (Hinshaw, 1994). Having said this, the finding of high rates of **co-morbidity** between ADHD and CD/ODD may indicate the existence of an additional major sub-type of ADHD and an externalizing behavioural disorder (Angold et al., 1999).

The evolution of ADHD into an educational issue

It is especially pertinent to note that the long evolution of the clinical and scholarly treatment of the ADHD diagnosis has reached a point where educational implications are clearly evident. One of the earliest currently known antecedents of the current diagnosis, Alexander Crichton's account of 'morbid inattentiveness' published in 1798, is cited as being a close resemblance to the current *Diagnostical and Statistical Manual of Mental Disorders (DSM)* criteria (Palmer and Finger, 2001). This early emphasis on the cognitive dimension of the perceived disorder is reflected to a lesser extent in George Still's 1902 paper in the *Lancet*, which described a congenital 'defect of moral control' (Anastopoulos, 1999; Barkley, 1990). Twentieth century attempts to characterize the condition have included Minimal Brain Dysfunction and Hyperactive Child Syndrome. In 1968 the APA produced the first standardized criteria of Hyperkinetic Reaction of Childhood (APA, 1968 [DSM II]). This gave way in 1980 to Attention Deficit Disorder with Hyperactivity (ADDH) (APA, 1980 [*DSM III*]), and was revised in 1987 to Attention Deficit Disorder (ADD) (APA, 1987 [*DSM IIIR*]). These changes are important because they reflect changing conceptualizations of the nature of the condition. The *DSM II* criteria marked a shift away from an emphasis on 'causation' to an emphasis on behavioural symptoms as the defining characteristics of the condition (Anastopoulos, 1999). This shift is reflected in the alternative diagnosis of **Hyperkinetic** Disorders (HD) (World Health Organization, 1990).

It is not true to say, however, as some commentators have, that the diagnostic criteria are simply 'behavioural' in their orientation. The diagnostic criteria require the clinician not only to make judgements about behaviours observed, but also to draw inferences about the cognitive processes underpinning those behaviours. Put simply, for the observed behaviours to be defined as symptoms of ADHD they must appear to the observer to be non-volitional. For example, impulsiveness, which is characterized by Barkley (1990; 1997) as the core feature of ADHD, cannot be observed, it can only be inferred on the basis of a belief about the extent to which a behaviour serves the interests of an individual actor. An impulsive act is defined as one that takes place without regard for the probable consequences of the act for the actor. It reflects an absence of forethought and planning. Furthermore, impulsive behaviour can be distinguished from, for example, hedonistic behaviour, by the relative inability of the impulsive individual to engage in the self-regulation of behaviour. The **hedonist's** behaviour is mediated by judgements about the pleasure that is calculated to accrue from an act. The impulsive individual's characteristic behaviour is defined by an absence of calculation. In psychological terms this represents a failure in the cognitive processes known as '**executive functions**' (Barkley, 1997) (see below).

This, along with other features of the ADHD criteria, should strike a major chord with educationists and others (such as parents) who have particular responsibilities for influencing the cognitive, social, emotional and moral development of young people. At its heart ADHD is concerned with the ways in which individuals engage psychologically with the world around them, how they regulate or fail to regulate their attention and behaviour, and how they respond to the efforts of others to influence their thinking and behaviour. In short, ADHD is at heart an educational issue.

This theme is developed more fully in Chapter 5 of this book, a central contention of which is that teachers' **pedagogical** decision-making can be significantly enhanced through knowledge of the nature of executive functions and their roles in pupils' engagement in learning tasks. Such knowledge is essential to understanding the particular needs of students with ADHD. The case of ADHD, however, provides valuable insights that are useful in understanding how *all* people think, learn and self-regulate.

Evidence base for ADHD: cognitive process

A definitive account of the causes of ADHD is not available. However, ADHD has become one of the most widely researched of all disorders of its type in the psychological and psychiatric literature. Tannock (1998), in an authoritative review of international research on ADHD, identifies three major areas of theoretical exploration of ADHD:

- cognitive research

- neurobiological research

- genetic research.

Evidence from studies in these areas provides a strong argument that ADHD is a bio-psychosocial condition, and one that requires a **multi disciplinary** approach to intervention to combine medical, psycho-social and educational dimensions.

Cognitive research has increasingly focused on impulsiveness as the central feature of ADHD, and the possibility that a dysfunctional response inhibition system is the neuropsychological mechanism, largely located in the physiology of the frontal lobes of the brain, underlying this problem. This neurobiological explanation is supported by a number of neuro-imaging studies (Tannock, 1998), as well as neurochemical studies which have detected dysfunctions in certain neuro transmitter systems implicated in the regulation of attention and behaviour (McMullen, et al., 1994). Further support to suggest that ADHD has a neurobiological foundation comes from genetic studies. Some have shown there to be a greater incidence of ADHD among identical (that is, monozygotic) twins than among non-identical (that is, dizygotic) twins, and among children who are biologically related as opposed to adopted (ibid.). Genetic research also suggests that ADHD may be a result of abnormalities in the **dopamine** system (ibid.). Dopamine is a neurotransmitter which is found in systems of the brain concerned with, among other things, the regulation of movement (Thompson, 1993). These findings suggest that children with ADHD are biologically predisposed to experience significantly greater problems than most in inhibiting or delaying a behavioural response, and therefore their impulsiveness is not under their control. An alternative view to the dysfunction of the neurobiological system in children with ADHD is proposed by Barkley (1997) as a failure of the inhibitory control system to become activated. Barkley (1997) suggests that neurologically based problems of response inhibition lead directly to problems in four major 'executive functions' of the brain which are essential for controlling self-regulation.

- The first executive function is *working memory*, impairment of which makes it difficult for individuals to retain and manipulate information for purposes of appraisal and planning.

- The second function is that of *internalized speech*. It is suggested that self-control is exerted through a process of self-talk, during which possible consequences and implications of behaviours are weighed up and internally 'discussed'.

- The third executive function is that of *motivational appraisal*. This system enables us to make decisions by providing us with information about the emotional associations generated by an impulse to act and the extent to which the impulse is likely to produce outcomes we find desirable.

- The fourth executive function is that of *reconstitution* or *behavioural synthesis*. The role of this function is to enable us to plan new and appropriate behaviours as an outcome of deconstructing and analysing past behaviours. Put simply, this executive function involves the retrieval of memories of similar situations to one currently being confronted, with a view to answering the question: 'On the basis of what happened on previous similar occasions to the present one, what are the likely outcomes of behaving in certain ways in this situation?'

It should be stressed that this and other models (for example, Sergeant, 1995; Sonuga-Barke et al., 1992; Van der Meere, 1996) apply almost exclusively to the hyperactive/impulsive and combined types of ADHD. The mainly inattentive type is believed to be caused by impairments in the individual's speed of information-processing and their ability to focus on or select the object for their attention. This contrasts with the impulsive/hyperactive and combined types which are believed to be underpinned by more fundamental problems that cause the regulatory functions to fail (Barkley, 1997).

In addition to the cognitive-neuroscientific evidence, there are data from a number of studies to suggest that factors in the family environment may be implicated in the development of

ADHD. Family factors include: parenting skills (Taylor et al., 1991); disorderly home environments (Cantwell, 1975); marital discord between parents (Barkley, 1990); maternal mental health and paternal personality factors (Nigg and Hinshaw, 1998). These findings, combined with the findings from neuro-physiological research, provide strength to the debate that ADHD is a bio-psychosocial condition, that is, a behavioural condition biologically predisposed. The biological predisposition and the behavioural outcomes, however, are mediated by environmental and experiential factors (Frith, 1992; Rutter, 2001).

Evidence base for ADHD: a bio-psychosocial construct

It is clear that ADHD is both influenced by biology and the social environment. ADHD is, indeed, Attention Deficit Hyperactivity Disorder 'socially constructed' (Purdie et al., 2002) in the sense that it is a diagnostic label that is applied to certain individuals. It is also socially constructed in the sense that the social environment is likely to have a powerful influence on the ways in which ADHD symptoms manifest themselves. Put simply, if an individual is prone to attention problems, has impulse problems or has difficulty in regulating his or her motor activity, there are certain settings that are likely to highlight these problems. Schools are such places. On the other hand, if the same individual finds him or herself in a situation requiring a great deal of physical activity, and where he or she is encouraged to pursue his or her own interests, there is a likelihood that ADHD-type symptoms will be less obvious, or even invisible. A bio-psychosocial explanation of ADHD would argue that, by virtue of their biological inheritance and social circumstances, some individuals are more prone to being constructed as being 'disordered' in this way than others. This does not mean that ADHD is 'caused' by biology; neither does it mean that ADHD is 'caused' by the environment. The most useful way of seeing ADHD, it is argued, is as the product of interacting biological and psychosocial factors.

An important aspect of this bio-psychosocial construct is the range of beliefs that individuals (that is, principally, children, parents and teachers) develop about it. Simplistic biological explanations, for example, may undermine individuals' sense of responsibility for doing something about the difficulties associated with ADHD, and may lead to an overreliance on medication as the sole treatment for the condition. Too much emphasis on psychosocial factors may lead to unrealistic expectations of what it is possible to achieve. A combination of the biological and the psychosocial **perspectives** allows for the acknowledgement of the fact that there are significant individual differences at work, one cluster of such differences being defined as ADHD. There is also the realization that the expression of these differences can be rendered more or less problematic by the social and environmental circumstances surrounding the individual.

ADHD and cognitive ability

The complexity of ADHD poses a challenge for studies attempting to measure the impact the symptoms have on cognitive ability. Studies measuring cognitive ability have been criticized as being methodologically weak and, therefore, their findings may not be conclusive. For example, Barkley (1990) suggests that children with ADHD have difficulty with verbal fluency, yet other studies suggest that the tests used to measure verbal accuracy are not semantically appropriate or age related (Fischer et al., 1990; Weyandt and Willis, 1994).

Further doubt that cognitive difficulties exist in children with ADHD is demonstrated by Lerner and Lowenthal (1994), who measured cognitive ability and found that 40 per cent of their subjects fell within the normal intelligence quotient (IQ) range. In a similar study, however, Songua-Barke et al. (1994) report reduced intellectual ability. However, Mariani and Barkley (1997) argue that studies showing poor academic performance in children with ADHD are identifying learning difficulties that were present from an early age and not as a secondary consequence of the condition. It is estimated that as much as 50 per cent of IQ is as a result of heritability factors, but that 30 per cent of the variance is due to a shared environment (Plomin et al., 1994). Therefore, tests that measure cognitive ability cannot report on intelligence alone; they also need to consider the role that the environment plays in learning.

Assessment and diagnosis of ADHD

The **heterogeneity** of ADHD along with its co-morbidity factors make diagnosis and management complex, but highlight the necessity for consensus over the assessment and management of this multifactorial condition. The importance of providing the correct diagnosis has seen assessment and diagnostic procedures undergo changes over the years (APA, 1980; 1987; 1994). As understanding about the condition has changed, the assessment criteria have moved from a continuum of symptoms to categories of symptoms. Along with these changes has come different guidance for professionals on how children with the condition should be best supported, from behavioural techniques to medication, with the more recent direction being a combination of the two (BPS, 1996; MTA Cooperative Group, 1999).

There is growing consensus among medical professionals throughout the world that in making a diagnosis of ADHD children need to be assessed using the American Psychiatric Association's *DSM IV* (APA, 1994) diagnostic criteria. The *DSM IV* criterion identifies 14 behavioural symptoms, which include physical, cognitive and emotional difficulties. The core symptoms required for a diagnosis of ADHD mean that children are diagnosed as being either the predominantly inattentive type, predominantly hyperactive-impulsive type or the combined type. In addition the symptoms must be pervasive across contexts and present before the age of 7.

What children, parents and teachers say about ADHD

The following case examples are taken from interviews with children diagnosed as having ADHD and from interviews with their parents and teachers. The extracts highlight how having different perspectives on the condition can give rise to different kinds of responses. The following illustrates the difference between useful and not so useful ways of thinking about ADHD.

Case study

The clinician who diagnosed Alan with ADHD has prescribed **psycho-stimulant** medication to reduce Alan's behavioural difficulties and make it easier for him to progress within school. However, according to Alan's mother, there is no improvement in his behaviour. As a consequence, she has moved him from one school to another in order to find a school that can meet her child's needs.

Parent: I took him out, I knew he was bright, but you just couldn't get him to sit and do it. He's settled (in the new school) but I am in every week, you know, it never changed, the pattern of his behaviour's never changed.

I said to him, 'Alan, why don't you realize these mistakes, you keep doing the same thing all the time, why do you keep doing it?' He says, 'Well, what it is, Mum, is when I do it, a little man in me head tells me, and I do it.'

When it [medication] wore off he's more hyperactive than what he was before, I think it's like withdrawal. He has twitching with his hands, and when he's sat watching the television it's worse. He's had it since about the third week he took the medication.

Teacher: He still has that, shouting out, and then realizing, 'I shouldn't have said that', but very often now if he does shout out it's something actually quite funny that he knows the rest of the class are going to enjoy.

I really am hoping that there'll be a statement, and that will give us funding to be able to watch him more in unsupervised times. I would recommend a SENCO, not just as class teacher but a SENCO, that's where his needs lie.

Child: If someone's just talking I can hear them, I can't think of my words and I can't concentrate because they're talking. I'd be writing my words and got it all in me head and they speak, talk right loud, then I can't concentrate and it's hard for me to think of them. Words won't have gone but I can't think, I can't think easy, because I just can't think as good.

I sometimes find it hard in my lessons, I can read the work but I just don't understand how to do it, and when I can't do it I get like all like tense.

I thought that I'd do better at school, I don't think that I concentrate better. My mum said that I was going to concentrate with the tablet, and I don't think I have, I just mess about.

I can't do anything, because the tablet, like, stops me. It sort of controls you, but I don't think it works hardly. I'm always cracking my knuckles, and I've started doing it when I'm watching the television. They make me nervous, my tablets, then I get aggressive.

Here we have examples of three different and often conflicting perspectives on the nature and causes of Alan's difficulties. The clinician adopts a biological perspective, seeing the underlying difficulties in terms of neurogical factors that can be controlled through the use of medication. The parent and child, on the other hand, see the problems as socially determined, and as residing primarily in the school setting with the teacher's failure to employ appropriate management and pedagogical techniques as a core problem. As far as the parent and child are concerned, the medication simply serves to exacerbate the problem. The teacher, however, adopts a psychological explanation, attributing Alan's disruptive behaviour to his desire to play the role of the class clown. What is striking about these different perspectives in their mutual exclusiveness. What is notably absent is any obvious attempt for the different parties involved to share their perspectives and co-ordinate their various efforts to improve the situation. Energy is being expended on blaming others, rather than attempting to co-construct solutions.

Case study

Jacques' mother sought a diagnosis for his behavioural difficulties and requested that the clinician prescribe her son medication to resolve the problems she and school were experiencing with his behaviour.

Parent: I had always said, if he's seeing too many people, it could be making him more confused than he is. He's seen a psychiatrist, then he went to see a paediatrician and an educational psychologist, and the social worker.

It needs sorting out, all this picking on him, because it's been going on now since he started school. They've always picked on him. Yesterday I got a phone call saying that he'd been disruptive, so I went in to see his teacher and he was saying that if he comes in school tomorrow morning he's got to go in [another class]. I don't think that's fair. So I kept him at home. I think they're just getting at him now because he doesn't see the child psychiatrist any more at hospital.

Teacher: He is disruptive, and in group work he's not very good at all. In science I put him in one group, there was a disagreement, and I had to take him out of that. I put him in another group, there was a disagreement, and I had to take him out of that. So he virtually worked with all the other groups, he was the catalyst and I suppose the others they wanted to get on.

This is the most annoying thing, he will sit there and he will tap his pencil on the table. Now if I'm on full form, I will ignore him and he stops, but obviously if it grates on me, then I will bite, and then I get the problem.

It's attention seeking basically. He's been seeing all sorts of different people, and I don't think he realizes what their purpose is, and he gets more and more confused, this is unsettling. And it's all attention you see, 'cos he's getting this attention.

Child: I thought doctor was going to take my brain out, so he'd put a new brain in that was good, but he was talking about my behaviour and my weight. He gave me little round tablets and they have made me lose weight.

Case study *continued*

I always get battered, all these guys in Year 6 and 5, so I batter them back.

Mr A hit my best friend, he pushed him so I hit him 'cos he was saying all sorts about me mum, so I smacked him, 'cos he shouldn't say things about my mum.

[I want my mum to say] That I'm good at school, but she never listens to me. Like when I tell her a story, she goes, 'Sshh', and tells me to shut up.

This case highlights how different perspectives about Jacques' behaviour affect the approaches used to address the problems. A lack of agreed understanding reduces the support in the home and in school, and the result is that the child's behavioural difficulties remain unchanged. Furthermore, we can detect an erosion of Jacques' self-esteem as a reaction to the frustration and irritation that others experience in response to his behaviour.

In summary, these case extracts highlight the need for ADHD to be understood as a bio-psychosocial condition, and for clinicians, teachers and parents to provide support structures that will enhance the child's social and academic development. Above all, is the need for the different 'stakeholders' to empathize with one another, and to attempt to reach a shared perspective which enables positive progress to be made.

Points to remember

The evidence suggests that there is no single cause responsible for the course and development of ADHD. Rather it is the interplay between genetics, the brain and psychosocial factors that influences behaviour. Although there is uncertainty in the literature as to how environmental influences contribute to ADHD behaviour, it may be that some children's genetic inheritance renders them especially sensitive to certain environmental influences. The implication for supporting children with ADHD is that clinicians, parents and teachers need to be aware of how the interplay between biology and the environment influences on the condition may operate in the specific case in hand, and how these factors impact on the child's social and emotional development.

Although it is important for readers to understand the symptoms and aetiology of the disorder, it is also important that these are considered within the context in which they appear. The next chapter attempts to demonstrate the reality of ADHD by exploring the experiences of living with the condition from the perspectives of children diagnosed with the condition, their parents and their teachers.

Key points to remember

Implications for good practice:

◆ Teachers and parents work together with the child to identify the child's strengths and limitations at home and at school.

◆ Inform the child of acceptable behaviour and boundaries.

◆ Inform the child of unacceptable behaviour.

◆ Involve the SENCO and classroom assistants in the partnership working.

◆ Keep instruction and guidance simple and consistent across organizations and disciplines.

◆ Keep partners updated of changes and involve the child.

The ADHD Experience

In this chapter we look more closely at what children, their parents and teachers have to say about the experience of having ADHD or living and/or working with a child who has the condition.

- ◆ An individual's experience
- ◆ Parents', teachers' and children's perspectives on ADHD
  - Case studies explored
- ◆ Looking at ADHD from different perspectives
- ◆ ADHD and medication: what do children, parents and teachers think?
  - Case studies
- ◆ The limitations of medication
- ◆ Key points to remember

An individual's experience

This understanding is important for a number of reasons, chief of which is our need to understand the realities of ADHD as they are experienced by those who live and work with the condition. Whether or not you, the reader, contest or accept the objective reality of ADHD, it is likely that you are concerned about the effects of ADHD on those who bear the label. Exploring the way the social environment impacts on the child with ADHD helps to clarify the thought process governing behaviour and the consequences this has on the way people think and respond.

A second important reason for caring about the perceptions of those who experience ADHD is that they have a right to be heard. All human beings have the inalienable right to have their voices heard. This is fundamental to a democratic society. Furthermore, the voices of the potentially or actually marginalized are a vital element in societies that aspire to social justice.

A third reason for listening to these voices is a technical one that relates closely to the two already mentioned. The *DSM IV* diagnostic criteria (APA, 1994) indicate that the information needed to make a clinical diagnosis, in part, relies upon data gathered from the first-hand accounts of children, their parents and their teachers. In addition, the *DSM IV* recommends gathering data from direct observation of the child. Behaviour rating scales, situation questionnaires, psycho-educational testing and medical evaluation are also used (McMullen et al., 1994).

Parents', teachers' and children's perspectives on ADHD

The cases that follow are taken from interviews with children diagnosed with ADHD, their parents and their teachers, and highlight some of the behavioural difficulties that arise in both the home and the school setting. (For more details at the data source, see Hughes, 2004.) The extracts suggest that in failing to consider ADHD as a bio-psychosocial condition, children's behavioural difficulties are exacerbated.

Case study

Padraig's mother explains that his school work has deteriorated due to bullying in school and that as a result he is a very unhappy child. However, although she believes that Padraig's condition has a biological origin she also believes that he is responsible for the way he behaves.

Parent: I get the impression that he can't be bothered. It's a lot of laziness. I think a lot of laziness. It's all, 'I don't want to do it. I can't be bothered with it'.

Padraig's mother interprets his lack of concentration as being laziness, but his teacher explains that in her view Padraig is preoccupied about what others think of him.

Teacher: The only reason he stands out from the others in the class is because he worries so much about what other people think of him.

The teacher suggests that he creates his own anxiety. She believes he has a negative perception of himself, and that this is reinforcing his negative view of others. She does not make the link between the bullying behaviour of Padraig's peers and his anxiety and low self-esteem. Padraig on the other hand is concerned as to why others view his behaviour as being 'silly', and is puzzled by their hostility towards him.

Padraig: Some people beat me up. It's been happening in school. A couple of days ago, every time I went outside all these boys jumped on me and started beating me up and said 'We'll be back to beat you up later', and then they pretend to go, but they're hiding behind the wall and I think, they're gone, so I go outside and then they jump on me. I cry, sometimes on my own. My mum says that I sometimes act stupid and that's why they tease me, but to me I'm not acting stupid, I don't think it's stupid.

In Padraig's case his teacher and parent believe that Padraig is responsible for his own difficulties, no consideration is given to the influence environmental factors might have on his behaviour. Teacher and parent have perspectives on Padraig's situation that conflict with his own, leaving Padraig isolated and confused, and, in the absence of effective self-management skills, all the more vulnerable to bullies.

This case highlights the importance of understanding behaviour and support being available in the child's school and home environment. It highlights the negative consequences of failing to consider the circumstances surrounding the problem behaviour and a failure to change them.

Case study

Amy's mother is concerned that, in school, Amy is blamed for problems that are outside her control and, as a result, she has become a scapegoat for the bad behaviour of others.

Parent: She's very sharp and this causes problems. For instance at school there was something in the playground that was wrong, it was started by another child, but Amy was the one that got caught and punished, that would make her react. She's not particularly naughty, it's because she reacts to things that normal children would ignore or pass by, she reacts to situations and makes it into a problem.

Amy's mother believes that her daughter is very sensitive, and as a consequence, this aspect of her psychological make-up leads to her overreacting to situations. Her teacher, however, takes a slightly more benign view, describing Amy as an 'astute' child who strives for perfection. The teacher suggests that in school her behaviour only deteriorates when she comes into conflict with people who do not know her, and are less tolerant of her individualism.

Teacher: There was an incident in the classroom, with another teacher, she [Amy] threw a book and went over and scribbled all over the board. She would never do that with me. She would never get to the point where she would feel she had to do that. The only problems I have with her are her calling out and being a pest sometimes.

This is a remarkably forgiving position for a teacher to take in relation to what most people would see as an extremely disruptive episode. For this teacher, Amy's disruptive behaviour in the classroom is not the result of malice, but is often the product of this highly intelligent girl's need for a high level of mental stimulation. In the case of the aggressive outbursts, these, she believes, are due to the way others respond to her when they do not understand this intense need.

In this case, Amy's teacher concedes that ADHD has a biological component, that makes certain aspects of her social and academic engagement difficult for her to regulate, but she is also considering the contribution social factors may have on her difficulties. For her, getting to know Amy's idiosyncratic ways, and finding a positive way of framing some of the things that make her potentially challenging to work with are key to preventing her frustration escalating into seriously disruptive behaviour.

Amy struggles to describe her own behaviour other then to say she was 'bad'. She referred to an outburst in school where she had sworn in the hearing of a lunchtime supervisor, who had mistakenly (according to Amy) thought she had sworn at her. By her [Amy's] account the supervisor had reprimanded her and she [Amy] had struck her. Amy's reasoning was that she had not sworn at her but at someone else, and that she was being blamed unnecessarily. She regretted hitting her but equally thought that she was 'getting her into trouble'.

Case study *continued*

Amy: I'm bad, 'cos I get in trouble a lot. I threw a book once, but I had asked Kate to
             move out of the way first so I didn't hit her. I wasn't aiming to hit anyone I was
             just aiming to wreck the classroom because we had a point taken off us for talk-
             ing in general knowledge quiz. But everybody else was talking, and nobody else
             got a point taken off them. It wasn't fair, 'cos everybody else was two and a half
             points ahead.

Amy claims her anger is a justifiable response to what she perceives as injustice. She attributes her aggression to the way others treat her, and she states that in a situation where she
is wrongly accused she will retaliate to defend herself.

In some ways, Amy's is an unusual case. First, on the basis of the teacher's account, it would
seem that Amy's class teacher is remarkably tolerant of her aggressive behaviour, especially
towards staff. The teacher's framing of these behaviours as the consequence of 'perfectionism',
indicates a real effort to understand Amy's difficulties from an educational perspective. To some
extent, this belies the mother's claim that the school adopts a blaming approach towards Amy.
Her class teacher clearly is not culpable here, though other staff and Amy's peers may be. A
second, unusual feature of Amy's case is her highly reasoned account of her behavioural outbursts. Both examples given here are justified by Amy in terms of a response by her to injustice.
The book-throwing incident is even described in terms that indicate it to have been a planned
act, carefully executed to avoid undesirable consequences: 'I threw a book once, but I had asked
Kate to move out of the way first so I didn't hit her. I wasn't aiming to hit anyone I was just
aiming to wreck the classroom because we had a point taken off us ... '. This could be highly
consistent with the teacher's view of Amy as a 'perfectionist', but it is not obviously consistent
with the core features of ADHD, which emphasize difficulties with self-regulation and a tendency to act without thinking.

Before we jump to the conclusion that Amy's apparent thought processes render her disruptive
behaviour as being not symptomatic of ADHD, we must bear in mind, on the basis of both the
mother's and the teacher's accounts, that Amy is a 'sharp' and 'astute' child. These qualities
make her extremely capable of providing justifications for her behaviour. As a 'perfectionist' she
may well have a vested interest in explaining her 'bad' behaviour in terms that protect her self-
image, even if this means inventing reasons for her behaviour after the event. The fact that she
repeatedly finds herself 'in trouble' suggests that she is not as in control of her behaviour as she
appears to claim. Her way of resolving the dissonance between her aspirations for perfection
and her 'badness' may be to invoke the injustice argument. Her argument is that she is forced to
be 'bad', because she is intolerant of injustice, of which she is repeatedly a victim.

Amy's case contrasts with Padraig's in two ways. First, Padraig appears bewildered, and acknowl-
edges that he has difficulty in regulating his behaviour. Second, whilst Padraig is clearly a victim
of the aggression of others, Amy is, even by her own account, aggressive towards others. Amy's
tendency to portray her own behaviour in rational terms that indicate a degree of self-control,
whilst this may not be as clear-cut as she claims, does offer opportunities for intervention that
may not be as readily available in Padraig's case. In so far as Amy is able to self-regulate, her
motivation to employ self-regulation is not aided by her current pattern of highly rational
self-justification. Her reasoning ability has the potential to be exploited by adults (especially

parents and teachers) to challenge the self-justification. A successful challenge may produce one of two outcomes. The first might be to undermine her current justification, and thus replace her distorted rationale with one which renders her misbehaviour irrational, and, therefore, cause her to modify it. On the other hand, if she is unable to exert an adequate degree of control over her behaviour, as her parent and teacher assume, then this will emerge as the appropriate rational explanation. If the latter were to happen, the way would be paved to support Amy with educational accommodations (for example, reducing the opportunities for her to become over stimulated) and cognitive interventions (for example, the teaching of cognitive-behavioural self-management techniques). See Chapter 5 for more details of these interventions.

In summary, this case is similar to the previous one in that the child's behaviour is subject to a range of different interpretations. In both cases the child is cast in the role of victim, though in the second case, there is a much greater sense of the child's receptiveness to rational explanations for her behaviour. In both cases there is evidence that there has been little active communication between the key stakeholders, which could have the effect of producing coherent accounts of the situations in which the children find themselves. Without this, it is difficult to see how effective intervention in the school and home settings can be achieved.

Case study

Abu's mother believes that people misunderstand her son, and that their negative attitude towards him can lead to him becoming frustrated and aggressive. She finds this misunderstanding reflected at home, as she and her husband do not share the same understanding of what they both see as Abu's difficult behaviour.

Parent: My husband will not accept that he's not just a naughty child and we have terrible weekends, because he believes he just needs a good smack, and Abu immediately picks up on this and reacts … His outbursts can last two hours, we have to restrain him, and when it's over he slumps and he'll say, 'I'm sorry Mummy', and he'll put his arms round me, and he'll sob; he'll sob his heart out.

This suggests that Abu's parents' different views about the cause and course of his behaviour are reflected in the different approaches they adopt for managing his outbursts.

Abu's teacher suggests that a lot of Abu's behavioural difficulties are due to his home environment and that Abu has learnt that unacceptable behaviour is tolerated.

Teacher: You know, it was very much [as if Abu says], 'I have moods, and tough: you've [got] to put up with me!' I believe there is some element of reinforcement from home, that such things are accepted. Obviously at school you try and encourage the children to become part of the 'norm' system, and to produce behaviour which is acceptable, rather than accepting unacceptable behaviour. Abu knows exactly what he is doing: he wants attention.

Because Abu's problems are seen by his teacher as being due to his 'attention-seeking' tendencies, she will not tolerate this behaviour within the class, and in order to discourage it she ignores him. A key feature of this perspective is the apportioning of blame. 'Abu knows exactly what he is doing', and manipulates situations in order to get people's attention.

Case study *continued*

Although the teacher believes him to be responsible for the behaviour, the teacher also believes that its origins lie in the home situation, where these behaviours are 'reinforced'.

Abu, by contrast, believes that he has difficulties in self-regulating his behaviour, and that this causes him to become violent. He believes that only medication can help him to control his temper.

Abu: I take my medication so I don't get very hyper. So I don't get to hit anyone in the class because if I do I get in bother. Medication makes it go away, because it's me temper – it just comes up. Don't know why – [maybe it is affected by] sweeties and that.

Whilst Abu believes that medication plays an important role in reducing his outbursts, this is not supported by his parents or teacher. With no consensus about the cause of his difficulties, Abu is on the receiving end of inconsistent attempts to manage his behaviour. Furthermore, the triangular conflict involving him, his father and mother can only serve to undermine his sense of emotional security. And although his mother appears to be sympathetic towards him, she also appears unable to convince other key players (her husband and the teacher) to share her sympathetic view.

In summary, this case identifies different perspectives about ADHD. The inconsistencies within the home and between parents and teachers exacerbate the child's difficulties, leaving the child to believe that medication is the only form of effective support, even though the other stakeholders appear to see little significant evidence of this effectiveness.

Looking at ADHD from different perspectives

These cases highlight how professionals and parents can each approach the child with the ADHD diagnosis from different and, sometimes, conflicting perspectives. There is often only a consensus in relation to the view that the child presents with disturbing behaviour. The explanations for the behaviours tend to reflect debates in the literature, with different views being expressed as to the extent to which the behaviours are within the control of the child, or are the product of biological or social influences. These differences in opinion tend to lead to different approaches to handling the child or, in some cases, to an abdication of responsibility. The lack of coherence between the views held by the different stakeholders results, in each case, in a failure to achieve a consistent and effective approach to intervention, which is a fundamental barrier to positive change. One of the most glaring issues that is repeatedly neglected is the way in which the failure to establish a shared view of the problems faced by the child contributes to an environment which exacerbates the problems. Even the more sympathetic responses tend to translate into patterns of blame, rather than positive intervention strategies. The children themselves tend to respond to these confusing circumstances with either a sense of helplessness or a tendency to blame others. In each of the three cases, there is a sense of an impaired self-image: the children feel helpless, 'bad' or guilty.

These brief cases suggest that almost regardless of the actual nature of ADHD, in terms of the origins of its core characteristics of inattentiveness, impulsivity and/or hyperactivity, the social context in which it is manifested is of enormous importance. In all three cases, the conflicting views surrounding the child are a source of distress and confusion, and as such they are barriers to improving the child's situation. If we add to this the assumption that, by virtue of each child being the bearer of the ADHD diagnosis, each child exhibits severe problems with two or more of the three core features of ADHD, then we can see how these difficulties are likely to be compounded by the failure of the adult stakeholders to engage in a constructive dialogue with one another and the child.

ADHD and medication: what do children, parents and teachers think?

We now move on to another important aspect of the experience of ADHD, which affects many children who bear the diagnosis. The following case studies taken from interviews with children diagnosed with ADHD, and their parents and teachers, highlight their views of the effects that psycho-stimulant medication have on both behaviour and learning outcomes. We also consider the impact of the ways in which they construe their experiences on opportunities for positive intervention. The cases illustrate how ideas about what medication is able to achieve have consequences for the options that teachers, parents and children believe they have for alleviating difficulties.

Case study

Rajiv seems unequivocal in his belief as to the effectiveness of medication for ADHD:

Rajiv: I will be very, very good then [when I have taken medication], sitting quietly, sitting sensibly. I'm naughty, only when me tablets have wore off. I need me tablets to stop me from being naughty.

Not only does he believe medication to be responsible for enabling him to sit 'quietly', which is probably an accurate behavioural observation, he also attributes more qualitative effects to the medication. This is reflected in his use of the words 'good' and 'sensibly'. It is medication, or its absence, that determines whether or not Rajiv is 'naughty'. This indicates a belief in the power of medication to control his behaviour directly, rather than its power to influence his ability to control his behaviour. The idea that he may have a role to play, in terms of his ability to make behavioural *choices*, does not appear to figure in his account, indicating little or no appreciation of the role of human agency and motivation in the process of behavioural self-regulation.

Rajiv's mother offers a different perspective to her son's school experience, and indicates to us that the medication has not always had the effects Rajiv describes:

Parent: He wasn't getting an education because every other day I was being phoned up telling me that he was too bad and I had to come and get him, the Ritalin and school just didn't seem to go together.

As a result, the mother has moved Rajiv to a different school.

From Rajiv's teacher's perspective, medication has had only a limited effect on his behaviour, and she believes that his difficulties are the product of neurological dysfunctions that are beyond remedy.

Case study *continued*

Teacher: Even with Ritalin his concentration is still poor. He is less hyperactive though. But I believe that Rajiv has physical problems that are in his head, and his characteristics are too embedded for any changes to occur.

For this trio, there seems to be one thing on which they agree, and that is that there is no role for Rajiv to play in overcoming his attentional and behavioural problems. We might infer from the teacher's comments that she, like Rajiv, places enormous faith on the power of medication to regulate Rajiv's behaviour. This faith is such that, according to Rajiv's mother, the school's major response to the failure of the medication to have a sufficient effect is to exclude the boy. Only the mother appears to have some sense of the importance of factors other than medication in the management of Rajiv's problems.

This case illustrates the way in which unrealistic expectations about what medication can achieve may restrict the range of options for intervention that might be considered. This theme will emerge repeatedly in the following examples.

Case study

Daley's mother suggests that medication has improved some aspects of his behaviour but there are problems due to the side effects of the medication, and she is worried about the long-term implications.

Parent: I worried when he first took them. He has had chest pains last month, [and] the doctor gave him a scan. Now they didn't think it was related to tablets, but he has pins and needles in his feet and that's a problem, and he's lost weight. Since he lost weight he's got paranoid about his bones, I mean his bones seem to be like sticking out but you know if he knocks his-self, and he's very sensitive.

Daley's mother attributes both physical and psychological problems to his medication, despite reassurance from the doctor.

Having said this, Daley's mother also tries to convince Daley of the need to continue with the medication.

Parent: I've explained and I've said that 'these tablets will make you lose weight but they are to make you good, do you want to be good?' and he said 'Yeah'.

This well-intentioned effort has the potential to exacerbate the psychological difficulties she believes Daley to have. On the one hand, he is experiencing anxieties regarding the side effects of the medication, and yet his mother is attempting to persuade him to take the medication. His refusal to take the medication is likely to be interpreted as a lack of desire to 'be good'. The benefit of 'being good' is his mother's approval, but the cost is deep concern about the physical effects of the medication. This is a classic 'double bind' situation, which is likely to increase Daley's negative feelings. Furthermore, the mother is, unwittingly, encouraging Daley to see himself as both dependent on the medication and, therefore, powerless in relation to his condition.

Case study *continued*

Daley's difficulties are further compounded, according to his mother, by what she sees as his teacher's insensitivity towards him, particularly in relation to the way that medication is managed in the classroom situation:

Parent: He doesn't like to be embarrassed. That does affect him if you embarrass him. And this is what is happening at school, when his teacher was calling him out to take his medication, that would make him angry, the embarrassment.

The public way in which Daley's medication is handled by the teacher is not only a source of embarrassment to Daley, but the embarrassment, in turn, leads to angry outbursts. This suggests that factors around the ways in which medication is portrayed and managed, both in the home and at school, actually exacerbate the very problems that the medication is intended to alleviate.

Daley's own attitude towards medication reveals a child who feels himself to be at the mercy of his medication, in relation to both his behaviour and his educational performance:

Daley: Sometimes the tablets work because sometimes they make me be good, but when they're not working I don't do any work.

Any sense of personal agency he may have had has been eroded by parental perceptions that place unrealistic expectations on the medication.

The view that medication alone has the power to transform the child's behaviour and academic performance, that is evident in this case, places a sensitive child in a highly problematic situation. For Daley medication is associated with two conflicting beliefs. The first is that medication has the power to correct the difficulties that distress his mother and himself: he can become the child both he and his mother want (and the student he and his teacher want) *only* through the taking of medication. On the other hand medication is, in his eyes, associated with serious physical side effects that threaten his health and emotional stress which is caused by the way in which it is managed in school. This complex of negative factors suggests that the benefits that may be associated with the medication, in this case, are offset and probably outweighed by the associated emotional toll.

Case study

Ivan's teacher suggests that, despite the medication generally having a calming effect on Ivan's behaviour, it does not stop some violent outbursts.

Teacher: He just started to go, just the odd time and his language was appalling and then this year, we've had various instants.

The teacher goes on to explain that it is not only those around Ivan who are disturbed by these outbursts, Ivan too is distressed by them:

Case study *continued*

Teacher: He curls up on the floor, in the sort of anger with himself and the situation, and then afterwards he's distraught and says he's sorry.

Ivan's difficulties are heightened by the conflicting influences of his distaste for medication tied to the belief that without it his behaviour will worsen:

Ivan: [I am sometimes] Swearing, trying to smash stuff, but I always do when I don't have my medication. My mum always thinks I'm going to go crazy and she wants me to take my tablets all the time, because sometimes I go over a certain limit and then I can't stop, and I'd be hitting people. I like my own space. I don't like people too close to me. It makes me angry.

As in Daley's case, Ivan is sensitive to his mother's anxieties about his behaviour, and aware of the importance that she attaches to medication as a means of controlling this behaviour. Daley's and Ivan's concern about taking medication is echoed in the next case study.

Case study

Luca, like Daley and Ivan, feels unhappy about taking medication. Like Daley, Luca dislikes the physical side effects of medication, which in his case involve his sense of vitality:

Luca: I don't like medication, because, I mean, I want my energy, 'cos I won't have enough energy to do anything – enough energy to go out and play football.

Furthermore, unlike Daley and Ivan, Luca does not believe that medication is effective in helping to manage his behavioural and attention problems:

Luca: I'm still naughty, even when I do take my tablets my room is a mess, and I forgot to tidy it. I keep trashing stuff because I get angry. I feel angry because my mum's going, 'Clean your room, clean your room' and then I go upstairs and don't do it.

The contrasting feature of Luca's case, with those of Daley and Ivan, is the sense that his active distaste for medication carries through into a reluctance to taking it. Furthermore, this resistance can be seen as reflecting a genuine sense of self-agency, which is reflected in his active efforts to self-manage some of the difficulties he believes himself to have:

Luca: I don't want to play with other children, people keep annoying me. I have friends, but I don't want to play with them, because I want to be on me own.

We may think of Luca's preference for solitude as a means of staying out of trouble potentially problematic in relation to his social and emotional development, however, we can also interpret this independence of thought and action as a positive quality that might be exploited to enable him to learn more pro-social self-management strategies.

No matter how we look at this case, Luca comes across as a child who has a sense of his own agency. He is not disempowered by the beliefs he has about ADHD, though he is concerned that he has difficulties managing his anger and sustaining attention to classroom tasks:

Luca: I get into trouble for not listening to the teacher. I get a time out sheet at least 20 times. But I do listen but then I forget because I'm doing something else. I was doing the tables and someone said stuff, and then I forgot what to do next, and then Miss sent me for a time out sheet.

Although we can see positive possibilities in Luca's orientation to ADHD, we have to acknowledge that these do not (according to his account) appear to be being exploited to positive effect in the classroom. Furthermore, there is an implication that his view of ADHD and how it should be handled is not shared by either his mother or teacher. This situation may add to the self-imposed isolation that is Luca's preferred approach to managing the difficulties he experiences.

The limitations of medication

As we have shown, many of the children and parents interviewed in this study expressed a very strong belief in the almost magical power of medication to improve behaviour. Even when this is the case, however, many adults also express concern about what they see as unwelcome aspects of medication.

Luca's mother believes medication has caused him to become sensitive and emotional; behaviour which makes him susceptible to emotional outbursts: 'This is the downside of the medication. He is already emotional but once he has had that medication, the emotions increase. So if someone antagonizes him he'll start crying, uncontrollably.'

Abu's teacher perceives that although medication has improved his behaviour, he believes that Abu's personality has been adversely affected.

Teacher: The one negative side is that he's lost his sparkle. He's quite a character and verbally he's got a lot to say. I think he knows a lot as well, he's got a good knowledge.

Padraig's mother believes her son has become dependent on the effect of medication in the management of his behaviour. She would rather he developed ways of coping without medication.

Parent: I think he's got this impression that if he doesn't have his tablets, he can't do anything. I said, 'Well, Padraig, you are going to have to try without thinking about, "I've got to take tablets or I can't do it". You've got to help yourself and not to rely on these tablets'.

The following example demonstrates the concern of one mother that medication is being used as a prop. She believes that the problems underlying her child's behavioural difficulties are not being addressed. She believes that ultimately it is the child who has to learn how to manage his behaviour.

Parent: I'm so concerned about his anger management, him doing something about himself. I don't want him just to rely on the medication. He just forgets things and he's kind of in a world of his own, he can't remember where he puts things, he doesn't know what day it is, he doesn't know what happened five minutes ago.

Yet another parent is concerned that her son is now seeking medication to avoid being told off: 'He might say something, say you're telling him off, "Well why don't you give me a tablet?"'

These extracts demonstrate that whilst medication is often seen as having the effect of controlling some of the surface features of ADHD, some adults express concerns over the limited effectiveness of medication in dealing with the underlying causes of the ADHD behaviours.

It would make life so much easier for all concerned if it were possible to create simple definitions for the things in our world, unanimous definitions that everyone could agree on. From the voices represented in this book we are already beginning to see the problems differences of opinion can course. Whilst there is an acceptance among many, though not all, of those interviewed that ADHD provides a valid account of the difficulties being experienced by the children in question, there are divergent views as to how the condition should be understood. There are those who opt for a straightforward biological explanation for the condition, and then there are those who adopt more social and psychological explanations. Similarly, where medication is part of the ADHD experience, whilst there is support for the belief that medication is a powerful and reliable intervention for ADHD, there are differing views about its wider effects on the children. There are concerns, for example, about the overreliance that some children may develop on the medication, and its assumed effects.

As we have seen, adults often play a leading role in shaping the beliefs that children develop about the nature of ADHD, and the power of medication. They do this in direct ways, by virtue of what they tell their children about these things (Hughes, 2004). They also influence their children in more indirect ways. When children are exposed to adults' sometimes conflicting perspectives and opinions, they tend to experience confusion and anxiety. This sometimes leads them to take desperate measures in order to 'be good', and to thereby cease being a source of trouble to their parents or teachers. Unfortunately, among these cases, confusion and conflict seem to be common denominators. In these circumstances, as we have seen, because of difficulties in achieving a consensus among stakeholders, there is a repeated failure to identify and implement constructive and coherent intervention strategies. In place of appropriate intervention we find confusion, anxiety, blame, guilt and an overreliance on medication.

Key points to remember

- ◆ Children's perspectives need to be heard, and understood, by teachers and parents.

- ◆ Combined support is required in home and school settings.

- ◆ Greater communication and shared views are needed between all parties.

- ◆ Understand the strengths and limitations of medication.

- ◆ Consider the wider environmental factors influencing behaviour.

CHAPTER 3

ADHD and Medication: A Brief Consideration of the Evidence

In this brief chapter we focus on what the clinical and research literature has to say about the use of medication for ADHD with a view to finding out if there are ways of resolving some of the difficulties that we have identified in the ways in which medication is constructed by some stakeholders.

- Psycho-stimulant medication
- How psycho-stimulants work
  - Some concerns about psycho-stimulants
- Medication and other forms of intervention : what works best?
- Implications: the value of medication as support for ADHD
- Key points to remember

Psycho-stimulant medication

A wide range of medications has been used in the treatment of ADHD. Teeter (1998) lists nine different drugs that are widely used in the USA. These can be grouped under the headings of psycho-stimulants, antipsychotics, tricyclic antidepressants and monoamine oxidase inhibitors. Of these, the psycho-stimulants are the most widely used in both the USA and the UK, and the most commonly used psycho-stimulant is methylphenidate, known by the brand name of Ritalin (NICE, 2002).

The development and refinement of methylphenidate have continued, and in 2001 a new slow-release version of methylphenidate (Concentra), and beaded-methylphenidate (Metadate-CD), was approved for use in treating children with ADHD. Studies evaluating the effectiveness of the new drugs show that behaviour improves over the school day (Greenhill and Ford, 2002). In addition, whereas Ritalin is effective for just three to four hours, these new drugs require just one dose given in the morning (rather than two or three times a day as was the case with methylphenidate).

How psycho-stimulants work

It was in the USA, during the 1980s, that psycho-stimulant medication became an increasingly widespread form of treatment for children with activity and attention problems. Psycho-stimulant medications, as their name implies, have the effect of stimulating brain activity. In particular, they increase the effective use by the brain of neurotransmitters (Teeter, 1998), deficient use of which is strongly implicated in neuropsychological theories of ADHD (see Chapter 1).

Psycho-stimulant medication has a direct effect on the posterior prefrontal part of the brain, reducing the symptoms of ADHD in 70 to 90 per cent of diagnosed children (Barkley, 1998). Children are reported to become less impulsive, less restless and less distractible, and exhibit improved short-term memory (Barkley, 1998). In so doing, psycho-stimulants reduce the core symptoms of ADHD, thereby enabling other therapies, such as **cognitive behavioural therapy** or social skills training, to be employed (Campbell and Ewing, 1990). It is also follows that effective use of medication facilitates more active, focused and sustained engagement with appropriate learning activities (see Chapter 7).

Some concerns about psycho-stimulants

The long-term use of the drug is of concern as there is evidence to show that although psycho-stimulant medication can produce short-term improvements of the type already mentioned, these improvements do not translate into long-term behavioural and academic gains (Klein and Mannuzza, 1991).

Despite controversy over the effectiveness of psycho-stimulants, it has been reported that their use in the USA and in the UK has increased. Between 2 and 5 per cent of all schoolchildren in North America receive pharmacological intervention for hyperactivity, with more than 90 per cent of them receiving methylphenidate (Greenhill, 1995).

The attractiveness of medication of this type is the immediacy of its effect, the apparent relative safeness, and its general reliability. However, concern is now emerging about the side effects of Ritalin, and studies have identified irritability, headaches, stomach-ache, motor and visual tics, difficulty in sleeping, and suppression of height and weight in some children (Schachar et al., 1997). In addition, mood changes have been found to accompany the taking of psycho-stimulants (Bohline, 1985; Buhrmester et al., 1992). Furthermore, the original form of methylphenidate which is active for only a few hours is characterized by a 'rebound effect' (Teeter, 1998). This means that in many children who take the drug, at the point where its effect wears off, the child's ADHD symptoms reassert themselves to a higher level of intensity than the child normally experiences.

Medication and other forms of intervention: what works best?

In the 1990s, the National Institute of Mental Health (NIMH) in the USA conducted a five-year comprehensive study into the effectiveness of treatments for ADHD, in six sites across the country. The study, 'The multimodal treatment study for children with ADHD' (MTA Cooperative

Group, 1999) found that medication is a more effective treatment for reducing the symptoms of ADHD than behaviour therapy on some, but not most, symptoms. The study identified that medication was more effective in reducing the major symptoms of ADHD than behaviour management. Classroom behaviour, social skills, social and peer relationships, and academic achievement were not as responsive to medication as they were to behaviour management strategies.

However, this study has been criticized for being methodologically weak, particularly in relation to the behavioural measures that were used. Also, the long-term effects of medication were not monitored and behaviour was not measured after medication was withdrawn, even though behaviour was managed after the withdrawal of behavioural management interventions (Pelham, 1999).

In a recent meta-analysis of 74 studies, Purdie et al. (2002) report that there is no consensus as to which of the main interventions for children with ADHD is the most effective. They conclude that:

> there were larger effects of the various interventions on behavioural than on educational outcomes. These overall effects were larger for medical interventions than for educational, psychological or parent training interventions, but there was little support for the reduction in behaviour problems to enhanced educational outcomes. (Purdie et al., 2002: 61)

These authors also argue that although medication serves to reduce hyperactivity, inattention and impulsivity, there is only a small improvement in children's cognitive abilities, and less improvement than when children participate in school-based intervention. They suggest that to achieve significant positive educational outcomes, educational interventions need to be adopted in a sustained and determined way: 'if we are looking to promote educational success among students with ADHD, we must use strategies that directly address their academic difficulties' (Purdie et al., 2002: 88).

Implications: the value of medication as support for ADHD

It is claimed that: 'Stimulant medication for children with ADHD has been the focus of more research than any other treatment approach for childhood disorders' (Teeter, 1998: 184). This is an important point to bear in mind, given the controversial nature of the issue of medicating children with behavioural problems. One vociferous critic of the use of medication for this purpose asks: 'Is [the use of medication for the treatment of ADHD] a cheap fix to avoid the necessity of questioning schools, parents and the broader social context of education?' (Rose, 2004: 7).

We might expect the vast body of knowledge that has been generated by thousands of published studies to help us to answer at least part of this question: is stimulant medication a 'fix'? The answer, based on our brief exploration of some of this research, is that medication offers a limited 'fix'. It can control some of the core symptoms of ADHD in the short term, but has limited efficacy over time.

Having established that medication can have a 'fixing' effect, albeit a limited one, we might now try to answer the question: is it a *'cheap* fix'? This is a more difficult question to answer. Changing children's behaviour is a complex and labour-intensive task, if adopted into a conventional educational system by schools, parents and therapists. For example, teachers in schools devote thousands of their working (and non-working) hours to devising and implementing strategies for managing and preventing deviant behaviour and promoting positive behaviour. Behaviourally challenging students are sometimes deemed not to be appropriately placed in mainstream classrooms, and require placement in groups with low pupil–teacher ratios, or even on a one-to-one basis with a member of staff. In some cases, children with these difficulties are placed in residential settings. These are very expensive educational provisions, far outweighing the cost of treatment with medication.

Having said this, we have to bear in mind what the ultimate goals of intervention for ADHD are. From the parent and child's point of view intervention should not simply result in the control of the symptoms of ADHD. Effective intervention should enable the child to benefit from his educational, familial and social experience in ways that facilitate his or her progress towards an independent, happy and productive life. If this is so, then we must conclude that methylphenidate may be able to play a small, though for some children, important part in the intervention process.

By controlling the symptoms of ADHD, the child is rendered amenable to the influence of good teaching, social training and interventions directed at emotional growth. For some children the medication is important because it opens the way for these kinds of influences. It is, however, the quality of these non-medical influences that is likely to be the most powerful aid to positive progress.

If we return to the cases presented in the previous chapter we can see not only do many of them have a distorted and inaccurate perception of the effects of medication, but they also have an unrealistic belief in the power of medication to transform children's lives. They often mistake the short-term gains they experience as an effective response to ADHD. In these circumstances it is not the medication itself that is the problem, rather it is the way in which the medication is perceived, and the effect this has in precluding other, highly necessary, forms of intervention. As we will see in subsequent chapters, there is far more to effective intervention for ADHD than medication alone, though it can play a part.

Key points to remember

◆ Side effects of medication are numerous.

◆ It is important to recognize both the positive aspects and the limitations which medication has on behaviour.

◆ In the short term, psycho-stimulants can control some of the behavioural symptoms of ADHD.

◆ Long-term behavioural and academic gain requires a combination of interventions.

CHAPTER 4

ADHD and Schools

In this chapter, we consider the relationship between ADHD and schools. Central to the discussion that follows is the issue of **inclusive education**. After an exploration of the meaning and implications of inclusive education, as it is commonly defined and operationalized, we return to the day-to-day experience of our case study children, their parents and teachers. The aim of this chapter is to examine the extent to which these pupils can be said to be 'included' in the schools they attend.

- ◆ Inclusive education – what does it mean?
- ◆ The experience of schooling
  - – Case studies
- ◆ The educational challenges of ADHD
  - – Should children with ADHD be in mainstream schools?
  - – Defining **educational engagement**
- ◆ Key points to remember

Inclusive education – what does it mean?

Children with ADHD often present a significant challenge to teachers in mainstream schools. For this reason some teachers are not unsympathetic to the demand made by some parents that their children should be educated in specialist schools for children with ADHD. There are, however, good reasons why this proposal should be questioned. The education systems in the UK have moved a long way since the 1940s when children who were deemed 'handicapped' were placed in segregated educational provision, under the direction of medical officers. Since the 1980s it has been a legal requirement that the education of all children should be in the hands of qualified educationists, and that educational provision for children and young people should conform to a common set of quality standards. This applies in modified form to children who are not in schools, owing to illness or because they are incarcerated.

This universal entitlement to a broad and balanced education means that children's educational needs are the primary concern when it comes to determining the educational provision that is made for them (DES, 1978). Within the logic of this framework, the presence of a formally diagnosed disability is only of educational relevance if it can be demonstrated to hinder a child's access to standard educational provision. In these circumstances, local education authorities (LEAs) are required by law to make additional provision, with a view to enabling the access to his or her educational entitlement. Where it is demonstrated that the extent of the additional provision goes beyond what can reasonably be expected of a mainstream school, LEAs are required to fund the child's placement in government-approved alternative provision, such as a special school or unit.

The positive side of this situation is that LEAs and mainstream schools have a duty to make all reasonable efforts to accommodate all pupils to a degree that enables them to take advantage of their entitlement to state-funded education. The down side of this laudable and socially just intention resides in the difficulties of deciding what is reasonable and adequate in terms of the level of access to educational services. Associated with this is the problem of determining when a school's and local authority's efforts are at an acceptable, adequate level.

This is a controversial area that begins with the agreeable contention that any society which values social justice and equality of opportunity must make social inclusion one of its primary aims. Furthermore, it is argued that social inclusion is achieved through the identification and removal of barriers to social participation that are experienced by socially marginalized groups and individuals. Education is a major sub-system in such societies. It is a vehicle for socialization, the development of individuals' sense of identity and the fostering of skills necessary for active, constructive and rewarding engagement in the local and global, social and economic community. It follows that an inclusive society must have, as a key component, an inclusive approach to education that prioritizes equality of educational provision and access to that provision (see Booth and Ainscow, 1998; Dyson et al., 2002; Sebba and Sachdev, 1997).

It is when we attempt to translate these highly desirable values and justifiable observations into policies that can be implemented in practical ways that we encounter difficulties. The major difficulty relates to how we define inclusive education. A highly dominant perspective equates inclusive education with the placement of children in their local mainstream schools. The argument that follows on from this is that although many mainstream schools have, at present, a limited capacity for meeting the educational needs of all the potential students in their immediate localities, they should work towards extending their capacity to include as many students as possible through the development of policies and practices that enable them to identify and cater for diversity. It is for this reason that inclusive education is often referred to as a 'process' rather than a 'state' (DfEE, 1997; Sebba and Sachdev, 1997).

The problem with this definition of inclusion is the difficulty that is created when attempts are made to put it into practice and to evaluate the effectiveness of the implementation.

Because inclusion is a 'process' rather than a 'state', an emphasis is placed on the progress that is being made in a given school towards becoming more inclusive. One of the most widely used tools for evaluating the effectiveness of a school's progress towards becoming more inclusive is the *Index for Inclusion* (Booth et al., 2000). This is a document that has been widely distributed amongst schools in the UK as a guide for developing and evaluating inclusive practices. The authors of this document state:

... inclusion is a set of never ending processes. It involves the specification of the direction for change. It is relevant to any school however inclusive or exclusive its current cultures, policies and practices. It requires schools to engage in critical examination of what can be done to increase the learning and participation of the diversity of students within the school and its locality. (Booth et al., 2000: 12)

Whilst this statement reflects a realistic view that mainstream schools differ widely in their current level of inclusiveness, the exclusive focus on mainstream schools as the major vehicle for promoting social inclusion is a serious flaw in the inclusion argument. Large-scale studies of inclusion tend to focus on the location of pupils, rather than the quality of pupils' educational experience (Norwich, 1993). Governments, and some researchers, seem to equate the success of their inclusion policies with the numbers of pupils placed in mainstream schools as opposed to non-mainstream settings. The smaller-scale studies that have focused on the nature and quality of the educational experience of pupils with special educational needs (SEN) in mainstream and segregated settings, on the other hand, present a more complex picture. For example, studies of students with social and emotional behavioural difficulties (SEBD) in the UK and the USA have repeatedly shown that small-scale, specialist provision is associated with the development of improvements in pupils' social and emotional functioning, improved educational engagement and higher levels of pupil satisfaction (Cooper, 1993; 2001)

It is important to acknowledge that there is evidence of some mainstream schools being successful in these areas too (Cooper et al., 2000), and more may be achieved as a result of *Every Child Matters: Change for Children* (DfES, 2003). However, at present most of the schools successful in including pupils with SEN, and in particular SEBD, are associated with low socio-economic status and social deprivation as well as low educational attainment (Cooper et al., 2000). Educational achievement is still highly correlated with socio-economic status (see for example, O'Neil Rand Corporation, 2005; Webber and Butler, 2006). The highest concentration of pupils with SEN therefore tends to be found in mainstream schools located in relatively socially deprived geographic areas. It follows that these schools have relatively low levels of academic achievement, which in turn make them unpopular with parents who have the cultural and economic capital that enables them to make informed choices about the schools to which they choose to send their children.

The problem with mainstreaming is that it assumes that so-called 'mainstream' schools share a quality standard and uniformity of educational opportunity that make them superior to non-mainstream provision. These are patently erroneous assumptions. In the UK, for example, the attainment gap between pupils in the best and worst state secondary schools, as measured by examination performance at age 16, indicates that pupils in the best schools are approximately five times more likely to achieve results that will qualify them to pursue an educational career that may lead to higher education than pupils from the so-called 'worst' schools. Furthermore, when we look at access to the most prestigious higher educational institutions, these will tend to draw their students from the most privileged schools.

These observations form the background to the rest of this chapter which considers the educational experience of those children who were the subjects of the research study reported in this book.

The experience of schooling

The children in this study all attended mainstream primary schools where it was clear, in most cases, that staff were aware of ADHD and believed that they were taking measures to foster the engagement of pupils with the condition (Hughes, 2004). There is evidence of teachers using contingency management techniques in the form of rewarding positive behaviour with tokens. Several teachers spoke about particular considerations that they had made in response to ADHD.

One teacher spoke about the particular need for firmness and consistency in dealings with the child with ADHD: 'If we show signs of being weak, when giving instruction we lose control over him.' Another teacher echoed this view, and cited the problem of consistency *between* staff: 'You've got to be firm, but also, he doesn't respond to some teachers in the same way that he does with others. He's fine with certain members of staff.'

The implication here is that the child with ADHD tests the school system and highlights weaknesses that may be applicable to all students. One teacher believes that teachers who do not exhibit the highest levels of professionalism in their student-management practices are exposed and undermined when confronted with a child with ADHD: 'I'm being unprofessional I know, but he knows the sort of weaker members of staff, and a supply teacher, when a supply teacher's coming in he'll rise to the occasion beautifully.'

The ironic use of the superlative 'beautifully' highlights the view that children with ADHD tend to respond to situations that most children find problematic in extreme ways. The same teacher went on to describe how well the student responded to her consistent approach, over time, and some of the measures she takes to cater for his particular need for routine and consistency: 'It took him virtually a term to settle down, get to know me, get to know the routine and accept it. Most of the time I try and keep [the need to deploy a supply teacher] to the same day and [try to keep to] the same supply teacher.' Implicit in this teacher's account is the need for teachers to show perseverance and to maintain a patient attitude. This echoes key recommendations from the literature on classroom management (see for example, McManus, 1989; Smith and Laslett, 1993).

It is interesting to note that teachers, in this study, place a strong emphasis on issues around the management of the behaviour of children with ADHD. As we will show in Chapter 7, from an educational perspective, there is a great deal more to providing appropriate pedagogy to the student with ADHD than simply managing his or her behaviour. One of the problems with this emphasis on management is the tendency for the student with ADHD to be characterized as problematic and to be singled out as requiring special treatment. As a result, even when the teacher's interventions are sensible and appropriate, the fact that the student with ADHD is subject to 'special' treatment can create problems of stigmatization. This was a particular concern to one parent who complained that, in using appropriate contingency management techniques, her son's teacher unwittingly exposed the child to ridicule from his peers:

> *The kids at school have seen him doing charts and things and they know and they treat him different now. It's a bad thing really, I think it's done nothing but cause problems. Well, the teachers made no secret of it. One of the first things was a good behaviour chart, which was a tick every 10 minutes of sitting still. But the kids picked up on it you see, 'Well we haven't got one of them.' And then the teacher explained to the class what his ADHD is.*

This parent is saying that whilst behavioural charts play a positive role in behavioural management, there is a failure here to give attention to the keen sensitivity of the child with ADHD. Low self-esteem is not a symptom of ADHD but has been found in many that are diagnosed (Barkley, 1990), therefore it is important that classroom techniques for monitoring behaviour acknowledge this, for example, by respecting children's privacy. In the example above, the teacher has objectified the child, by explaining to the class why his behaviour was being monitored. From the child's perspective this served to draw attention to his difficulties and has led to feelings of alienation (Hughes, 2004). This example highlights how easily a teacher can draw attention to the child's difficulties, making a particular behaviour – sitting still – and the reward – a tick – the focus for the child and the rest of the class. An alternative approach might have been for the teacher and child to consider a monitoring tool that only they are aware of. It may be that a tool is appropriate for one child, and not another, or that this changes depending on the behaviour being modified. In this way it gives the child an element of control, and maintains his or her privacy, whilst avoiding a negative (naughty boy/girl) situation exacerbated by onlookers.

From an educational perspective, we might also question why it is only the child with ADHD who is given rewards for appropriate behaviour. It can be argued that if schools and teachers routinely employed such strategies with all students, instead of reserving them for 'problematic' students, some of the difficulties that children with ADHD commonly encounter in schools would be prevented from occurring in the first place. Reserving such interventions for certain students is counter-productive. One of the hallmarks of the genuinely 'inclusive' school would be to make routine use of such interventions for all students.

Unfortunately, according to the parents and children in the current study, the absence of effective preventive measures meant that problematic situations tended to escalate, sometimes leading to exclusionary measures. One parent describes a scenario that is all to familiar to parents of children who exhibit ADHD-type problems in school:

> They [that is, school staff] called me at home. In the end four teachers eventually managed to calm him down. I don't know how long it took, but you could tell the teachers were upset about what had gone on. But I think they'd gone about it all wrong. 'Cos once he gets past a certain point, he can't bring himself back.

In this case, both the parent and child expressed the belief that behavioural outbursts were avoidable when appropriate preventative measures were in place. The mother had observed that when the boy became embarrassed he preferred to withdraw from the public situation. However, in the incident described above, the child was prevented from withdrawing. As a result the situation escalated, with the child becoming increasingly distressed and disruptive, and requiring several members of staff to intervene. The boy's own account of this incident is illuminating:

> I was angry in class, and I just went out of the classroom and then I got stopped and that made me even angrier. Miss tried to stop me, so I started hitting her arm so she'd get off me, I wanted to go home. I just felt really annoyed and started shouting when they come near me, I just snap at them.

His behaviour is explainable in terms of an impulsive response to a highly stressful situation.

From the teacher's perspective, there are a number of issues to consider here. First, she is faced with a child who is prone to aggressive outbursts and disturbing the class; secondly, she has a duty to the class and to the school to get through the day's workload.

> *It's just not worth it, for the speed of the lessons, I mean, we still have a curriculum to deliver, and in order to get through that we're having to move on, we're having to keep speed up to do our job, to be honest, to do teaching.*

The teacher's attempt to avoid confrontation can be understood, as this would not only exacerbate the child's outbursts but would disrupt the class and the lessons. However, an important lesson from this example is that responding to the boy's behavioural needs when they have escalated is too late to avoid confrontation and disruption. The consequences of this kind of approach for the child experiencing difficulties were very negative, and as a result serious problems were created for the teacher and the other children in the classroom who witnessed the confrontation. An alternative would be a proactive approach whereby, in times of escalating tension, a strategy agreed by other members of staff and the child could be implemented. This would avoid placing the teacher in a situation that calls for a reactive approach and placing the child in a confrontational environment that exacerbates behavioural difficulties.

Another mother described the way in which reactive, as opposed to preventive, approaches to her child's difficulties led, in her mind, to deterioration in the child's behaviour. She expressed concern that support provided by the school was inadequate:

> *He gets little bits of help when something goes wrong at school, it's like, 'Oh well we'll call in this person and we'll see what they can do.' And either nothing comes of it or else they'll do it a bit and say, 'Well we've done everything we can now.' But it doesn't change him. I'm not happy with his behavioural management because he's been referred several times at school to [a named member of staff] but nothing seemed to work at all and their involvement wasn't consistent.*

As in the previous example, the strategy used implies that the child's behaviour resulted from internal factors. The possibility that factors in the classroom might have triggered or exacerbated the behavioural problems was ignored. Yet, attempts to 'fix' the child's difficulties by referring him to a teacher outside the classroom situation seem to have had no positive impact. The more such interventions fail, however, the more intractable the child's difficulties appear to be. The frustrations experienced by staff, parents and child in these circumstances are likely to lead to an escalation of the difficulties.

Here again is an example of reactive approaches resulting in escalating behavioural difficulties. One of the themes running through reactive responses to an outburst or managing the child's behaviour is a lack of understanding about the cause of the outburst. In most cases the cause is ignored, being put down to the child's behaviour and ADHD. Therefore the response may be inappropriate for the behaviour and misleading for the child. One way round this would be to have a clear strategy that can be applied to any given situation, so that this brings about a swift resolution, and to have as part of that strategy an opportunity for the child (and other parties involved) to talk to the teacher at a later, more convenient, time about the incident in more detail. The lines of communication are an important tool by which to obtain a full picture from all parties and to understand where the problems lie. In addition, a clear communication strategy gives the child an opportunity to raise his or her concerns and to understand how his or her difficulties will be supported.

The following case studies illustrate the negative effects of seeing ADHD as an entirely within-child problem, rather than an educational challenge. This leads to children feeling marginalized and frustrated and highlights how this, in turn, exacerbates their behavioural difficulties.

Case study

One mother suggested that her son, Abu, was particularly sensitive to changes in his daily routine:

Parent: My problem is that every time he moves class we get the same problem. He can't settle, because he doesn't like change. It's the same at home but if he can decide where we go, he's happy.

Implicit here is the idea that Abu experienced a sense of dislocation and insecurity when placed in unfamiliar circumstances. Associated with this were memory difficulties, and problems he displayed in comprehending instructions:

Parent: Abu can't listen, it isn't that he doesn't listen, he doesn't hear what they're saying, he doesn't take it in. If they say, 'Don't do that', he stops, two minutes later he's forgotten, so he does it again.

His mother pointed out that this problem persisted in spite of the fact that he was taking medication. Her chief concern was what she saw as the school's need to be more sensitive to things that cause him distress.

On the other hand, Abu's teacher was frustrated with his erratic behaviour in school and was concerned that he was not achieving as well as he could:

Teacher: He can do work, but he ought to be beyond the level that he's at, that's my major worry at the moment. He's capable of a lot more than he's doing because his work's very variable and I think that does depend on his attention, and it depends on his interest in the subject at that particular time.

How can a connection between the teacher's assessment of the situation, and the mother's concerns about what she perceives to be Abu's needs, be made? There seems to be a consensus about the view that the symptoms of ADHD were at the root of his learning problems. The teacher could have tried:

■ discussing her concerns with the child's parents, as through an open dialogue they could have identified how insecurities affect his behaviour and identified ways to minimize these

■ providing the child with clear and repeated instructions to reduce his tension and apprehension

- identifying through dialogue with the child activities that interest him, and used these as a reward and an incentive to shape his behaviour.

Abu's erratic performance could so easily be mistaken for a lack of interest or motivation. This points to the importance of teachers getting to know the individual characteristics of students, so that they can appropriately interpret a student's needs.

Case study

An example of what happens when there is a failure to communicate knowledge of this kind is provided by a girl called Amy. She was highly critical of a supply teacher, and annoyed with her for making her rush her work, and for not explaining in a way that allowed her to understand the task:

Child: We had a supply teacher and we were doing science. We were writing these things down and she was telling us to take our time but she was rushing us. She was saying everything really quickly. I've never had anything finished since beginning of yesterday.

It is evident from Amy's comments that she was motivated sufficiently to want to complete the set work, but frustrated that she was unable to do so.

Interestingly, Amy contrasts this experience with the positive way in which the permanent teacher usually manages such situations. This points to the importance of teachers sharing their knowledge about individual differences among students. So, for example, the class teacher or SENCO should brief the supply teacher about how best to support the child; similarly, the supply teacher should brief the teacher after her session.

Even though Amy is complimentary about her usual teacher's approach to teaching, even this teacher is not always successful in facilitating Amy's effective engagement with certain learning tasks:

Child: Well, in maths, I get bored 'cos I'm a slow worker, I just get a bit bored and then I start to do my work slowly and then I get really, really bored. In maths I feel like a beginner and that bores me.

Here Amy's account suggests that she finds maths a particularly challenging subject, because she feels like a perpetual 'beginner' in this subject. For her, maths is a laborious and unrewarding subject that leads to feelings of boredom and, by implication, disengagement. When taken with her comments about being frustrated in her failure to complete the science task, we can see a picture emerging of a student who is motivated to learn when she is given tasks that she can manage in her own time and that enable her to experience some degree of progress.

Such an analysis could be used to provide the teacher with some insights into what she might do to help Amy engage more effectively with maths. A good starting point would be to identify her current level of functioning and to ensure that learning tasks are designed to fall within this area of competence initially, and then by increments, to extend her knowledge by scaffolding more complex tasks based on her existing competence. Such an approach to pedagogy depends upon the teacher taking a detailed interest in the student's individual approach to learning, and upon existing progress. This can be done by working in conjunction with the school's SENCO (Hughes, 2004).

Case study

One of the difficulties which students with ADHD commonly experience is commitment of their thoughts to paper. A boy called Padraig illustrates this problem. His mother, when interviewed, expressed deep concerns about this.

Parent: All his teachers, from him starting school, they've all said the same. He'll have views on things, and his reasoning's good, but trying to actually document this, you know, he just finds it so hard to write it down.

Padraig too was concerned with his work especially at his slowness in class. He described how he tried, unsuccessfully, to keep up with others, and how he found that he had to rush his work in order to avoid being told off.

Child: My heart starts beating because I might get in trouble for not finishing my work. I know it sounds silly, but I want to be ahead of people, and not finishing an hour after they're all finished. Like in my English, I've only got on to question five, when everyone else has got on to a really high question like 16. I'm not finding it hard, it's just I'm slow.

Once again, we have the image of a child who is motivated to succeed, but who feels that he is not succeeding. Furthermore, the reference to his increased heart rate suggests that he experiences extremes of stress, because of this situation. His own account cites fear of punishment as a key stressor. We can also detect signs of anxiety in the mother's account of her son's difficulties. She and he also provide some hints as to how his teachers have tended to construe Padraig's difficulties. They appear to be, on the one hand, perplexed at the disparities in his performance whilst, on the other hand, using punishment as a means of encouraging speedier progress. The combination of punishment and stress suggests that not only is Padraig not achieving his full potential, he is becoming upset and self-conscious about falling behind in class. We can only speculate on the long-term effects of such experiences on Padraig's motivation and engagement with schooling, but if this experience can be avoided then it would benefit all concerned.

Case study

Parents, too, can sometimes be unforgiving in the ways in which they construe ADHD symptoms. This was evident in an interview with the mother of a boy called Yuan, who was clearly frustrated with her child's behaviour, and blamed him for what she saw as a lack of motivation:

Case study *continued*

Parent: He just doesn't want to concentrate. He'll rush things so that he can go and do something else, like play on the computer. But even if he is sitting down, he's not sitting still, and he's not quiet. It just wears you down.

Similarly Yuan's teacher was concerned with Yuan over-focusing on some aspects of his work, whilst under-focusing on others. She believed this, plus his constant need for approval, meant that Yuan was capable of doing the work but that he chose only to concentrate on what he preferred to do.

Teacher: He can become quite fixated on what he thinks should be an answer to a question. If he is doing a piece of work he will decide himself, from maybe partially listening to an explanation, or having a preconceived idea of what the question was about, then he'd decide that's how he was going to work and what he was going to produce. So although he's got good ability, he can give a completely wrong answer to a question.

The teacher recognized that Yuan had a reasonably high level of ability, but believed he employed this in a selective way, according to his mood. She interpreted this as a lack of motivation. Thus Yuan's difficulties, which conform to well-known features of ADHD, are compounded by the blame that is being heaped on him by both parent and teacher.

An alternative approach might help both parent and teacher to support Yuan. For example, they might have discussed:

- the tasks that motivate the child, and whether these could be used as a reward, linked to the completion of activities that the child finds less engaging (Chapter 7)

- task avoidance being a fear of failing more than a lack of motivation, therefore encouraging the child to over-focus on tasks he can accomplish; teachers' and parents' awareness of this can offer the child greater support on tasks that appear to cause the child difficulty

- whether it is a particular task that is difficult for the child or whether their understanding or surroundings could be to blame?

The educational challenges of ADHD

It would be easy to read the extracts presented above and to conclude that the children in this study were particularly badly served by their schools, and sometimes by their parents. The children were often subjected to blame and made to feel guilty about difficulties that were beyond their control. In spite of this, they retained a high level of motivation for school work and a clear desire to succeed in terms that would please both their teachers and their parents. When we look at what the parents and teachers told us about the broader contexts in which they operate, we can appreciate the dilemmas they are confronted with. When parents transmit their own anxieties to their children, these anxieties are often borne out of care for the child and his or her future. They want their children to succeed and are frustrated, and sometimes bewildered, by the signs that their child is failing. Similarly, teachers are always motivated by the desire for their students to be successful. This is, perhaps, particularly so when they see evidence that students have abilities that are not reflected in their performance. Teachers also experience additional stressors in the form of external performance targets (for example, standard assessment tasks (SATs) results; performance league tables), as well as the daily challenge of dealing with large numbers of students, the majority of whom are easier to teach than the child with ADHD.

As we will see in Chapter 7, there are many things that teachers can do to support students with ADHD in classrooms. However, before they can employ these interventions effectively, they need to know something about the nature of ADHD, and the ways in which ADHD is influenced by environmental factors. They also need to get to know students as individuals. This is where teachers and parents working together becomes important. When they pool their knowledge of the child, they will find clues as to how best to engage with the child.

We will now turn to a key educational question that nearly all parents of children with ADHD will ask at some time.

Should children with ADHD be in mainstream schools?

In one sense the answer to this question is a straightforward and unequivocal 'yes'. In so far as all children between the ages of 4 and 19 in the UK have the right to free education in state-run schools, all children have the right to attend a mainstream school including, under the terms of the 2001 (DfES, 2001a) SEN and Disability Act, those with special educational needs and disabilities. In reality, of course, many children do not attend mainstream schools. Approximately 7 per cent of children in the UK are educated in the private sector. Some 2 per cent of children are educated in specialist provision, such as special schools' pupil referral units (PRUs), young offenders' institutions and medical facilities. The 0.1 per cent of children who are formally and permanently excluded from mainstream schools as a disciplinary sanction may appear in many of these institutions, though some will find places in other mainstream schools.

We must ask ourselves why it is that schoolchildren might find themselves in any one of such a wide range of educational settings. Clearly, private education is a matter of parental choice. There are many social and academic advantages to be gained from private education. For example, approximately 50 per cent of the undergraduate places at Oxford and Cambridge colleges are occupied by students who come from the 7 per cent of all children who attend private schools.

The simple fact is that a proportion of parents choose not to send their children to state-funded neighbourhood schools. They choose schools, in preference to the local ones, that they consider to be, for various reasons, advantageous to their children in terms of the educational opportunities offered. This does not only apply to the financially well-off parents who select privately funded provision. It applies also to the many thousands of parents who seek placement in state schools that share the same status as their local schools, but which they believe offer a better quality of education. These will include specialist schools which cater for children with particular aptitudes and aspirations, for example, those secondary schools that specialize in science and technology, modern languages, sports and business education.

This is not to say that we are advocates of specialist schools for children with ADHD. We, like the parents of children with ADHD, are in favour of placing children who have serious problems that reflect the symptoms of ADHD in educational settings that maximize opportunities for these children to engage actively and constructively in the social and academic life of the institution. This view is not incompatible with the concept of inclusive education. Whilst, however, inclusive education is increasingly equated with the *location* of children, we are concerned with the *quality of the social, emotional and academic experience* had by the child. For this reason, we prefer the term 'educational engagement' to that of inclusive education (Cooper, 2006). This means that where mainstream schools are appropriately orientated to meet the needs of the child with ADHD, they become the appropriate setting for the child. Where this is not the case, however, alternative forms of provision may be preferred. This may involve the use of alternative provision within the mainstream schools, such as a learning support unit or nurture group, or off-site provision, such as a pupil referral unit or special school (see Cooper, 2001). These alternative settings, when at their most effective, operate in concert with mainstream schools, and are explicitly designed to enable the child's partial and then full-time return to mainstream classes, when this becomes appropriate.

We have shown already that the children in this study often had difficulties in accessing appropriate educational experiences in their mainstream schools. There is no reason to believe, however, that they would have received more appropriate teaching and management were they to have attended an alternative form of educational provision. The crucial point being made here is that the best form of education for any student is the setting in which their social, emotional and learning needs are most fully met. This is what we mean by 'educational engagement'.

Defining educational engagement

Educational engagement can be defined in terms of active and constructive social and academic involvement in the educational process (Cooper, 2006). As has already been noted, mainstream schools sometimes have difficulties in providing opportunities for this kind of engagement. Survival in the mainstream school, for many pupils, depends on the development of resilience. For some pupils this resilience can be helped to develop through the provision of specialist teaching, sometimes in a specialized (that is, non-mainstream) setting (see Cooper, 1993; Cooper and O'Regan, 2001a).

Genuine educational engagement takes place when students are known, acknowledged and valued as individuals in the educational setting. The ethos, structures and practices of the institution create opportunities for all students to participate constructively both socially and academically. This contrasts with the experiences of many young people who are defined as having social, emotional and behavioural difficulties, who often describe their mainstream educational experiences as being characterized by de-humanizing and exclusionary practices (Cooper, 1993; Cooper et al., 2000; Schostack, 1982; Tattum, 1984). Such negative experiences lead to a sense of marginalization and alienation that easily converts into disaffection and withdrawal or active rebellion. The placement of such students in settings where they are valued and treated with respect be they mainstream (Cooper et al., 2000) or non-mainstream (Cooper, 1993) can have a dramatic and positive impact on students' sense of self-worth, motivation for positive social engagement and academic performance.

Furthermore, educational engagement has a cognitive dimension. Marjorie Boxall, the founder of 'nurture groups' (Bennathan and Boxall, 2003), has a very useful concept that helps us conceptualise what is at the heart of educational engagement. She refers to 'the organisation of experience'. This strand of the Boxall profile is broken down into five sub-skills.

Educational engagement (Bennathan and Boxall, 2003):

- gives purposeful attention
- participates constructively
- connects experience
- shows insightful involvement
- engages cognitively with peers.

Children who score high on these items show interest in classroom activities and other people, and engage actively and positively with educational experiences and other people. They are alert, empathic, purposeful, self-motivated, able to engage in sustained thought, and are unafraid of new experiences. They are adaptable and flexible (Bennathan and Boxall, 2003: 10–11).

When thinking about inclusion focusing on educational engagement (in the ways suggested above), it follows that we should ask serious questions about the setting in which the student is to be 'included'. If, in the case of the student experiencing ADHD (or any form of SEBD), the circumstances do not actively support and promote the individual's social, emotional and cognitive engagement (as we saw above in case studies of children with ADHD), then it is not providing an inclusive experience. In so doing it is at least helping to maintain, and is probably exacerbating, existing difficulties. On the other hand, settings that support and promote these kinds of positive engagement are, by definition, inclusive.

If we place social and academic engagement at the heart of educational and social inclusion, it follows that students are best placed in educational settings where they have access to, and support for, maximum social and academic engagement. There is no simple formula here, in terms of provision. For some students this will mean having access to a variety of forms of provision. Placement decisions should be based on a detailed analysis of the individual's needs, and the capabilities of the specific available provision options to meet these needs. This means that no single type of provision should be favoured over any other except in terms of its ability to provide opportunities and support for social and academic engagement.

In this chapter we have explored the educational experience of a group of students with ADHD. We have also considered issues surrounding the inclusion of students with ADHD in mainstream schools. Many of the problems identified seem to flow from assumptions that have been made about the nature of ADHD and the characteristics that are sometimes attributed to children with this diagnosis. An outcome of thinking about ADHD in a negative way is that these children appear to pick up on this and it causes them intense concern and anxiety. There is clearly scope for more positive ways of thinking about ADHD to be developed as a basis for more supportive interventions.

Key points to remember

◆ A preventative (proactive) strategy for dealing with the behavioural challenges posed by the child with ADHD may help teachers to avoid using a reactive approach which can lead to inconsistency and cause the child increased anxiety.

◆ Avoid changes to the child's routine and environment as this may help reduce their anxiety.

◆ Providing the child with subtle support during periods of unavoidable change by involving them in the process may help them adapt more easily.

◆ Provide a reward system for appropriate behaviour for all children as the 'norm'. This avoids children with ADHD being perceived as problem children.

The Necessity of Collaborative Working

In this chapter we focus on what key stakeholders believe to be appropriate and desirable forms of support for the child with ADHD. A particular theme of the chapter is the need for schools and teachers to work with other professions, and how teachers can best support and guide parents, who in turn can support and guide their child.

◆ Perceptions of effective support

◆ Environment and medication

◆ Practical classroom support for children with ADHD

◆ The need to work together

◆ Involving the child in collaborative working

◆ Evidence of collaborative working

◆ Making collaborative working work in your school

◆ Suggestions of what to do in your school

◆ Key points to remember

The following examples, taken from interviews with children diagnosed with ADHD, and their parents and teachers highlight the importance of collaborative working for reducing the negative consequences of ADHD. These accounts also draw attention to the types of support required from parents, medical professionals and educational professionals.

Perceptions of effective support

Case study

In our first example, involving Padraig, we find a convergence in the thinking of parent and teacher as a key feature of Padraig's difficulties. Padraig's mother believes that Padraig needs to remain calm in order to enable him to complete a task:

Parent: When he can't do something, he's angry, like tying his shoelaces and he says in an angry voice, 'I can't do it, I can't do it'. I'll say, 'Well just calm down, just try'. He wants to do everything in hyper speed.

The mother suggests that Padraig is reluctant to slow his pace down, which she believes would enable him to focus more effectively on tasks. She believes Padraig needs encouragement with tasks to enable him to improve.

Padraig's teacher also recognizes that Padraig has difficulty focusing on tasks, and suggests that a structured environment is required when he is working. She has found that when he is given verbal instruction he performs best when given only one instruction at a time, otherwise he forgets what is expected of him. She believes that for Padraig to function well in class, he needs consistent and 'uncluttered' information, with minimal distraction – similar support to that needed in the home.

Padraig finds that he has difficulty comprehending what is asked of him and although he receives help from people he would like further assistance.

Child: Sometimes the teacher gets people to help me, and sometimes she helps me. I try to learn it myself and sometimes my Mum tries to learn me, but it's like I don't take it in.

Padraig blames his inability to comprehend information and his difficulty staying on task on his poor concentration. However, he finds his concentration is less problematic if he is involved in a piece of work that interests him.

Child: I have difficulty concentrating. I've tried to be moved onto a table on my own, I've tried to be moved into a separate place so I can work better, and I've tried everything but I still find it hard to concentrate. The only thing that I can concentrate better on is drawing.

Padraig recognizes his limitations with tasks, but has learned that when engaged in a task of interest, like drawing, his ability to concentrate is not a problem. In addition, Padraig believes that his behaviour would improve if people accepted him and his limitations, and treated him with respect. He shows considerable insight when he identifies his own need to be viewed in terms of his strengths and qualities, rather than in terms of his failings. As we saw in the previous chapter, Padraig is a highly motivated individual:

Child: I hate people saying that I'm thick, I want them to say, 'You're a fast worker'. I want to be, well not praised, but I want to be just the same as the other pupils. I want to be good at my maths, know my times tables – I only know a couple of them – fast at writing, better at listening. Well I do listen, but I don't really understand.

Padraig has clear ideas of what he wants; he wants to improve and be accepted. The main obstacle seems to be obtaining support with his poor comprehension, and a persistent lack of respect from others. In an attempt to overcome his difficulties and keep up with others, Padraig often rushes to get through his work.

As is commonly the case for many of the children in this study, Padraig's situation is made complex by the competing demands of the various influences in his life. His mother, understandably, believes that if he can be kept calm and if he avoids situations that make him aggressive, his behaviour will improve. She finds that the escalated pace he apparently prefers to keep throughout the day makes keeping him calm difficult to achieve. His teacher also recognizes that Padraig's environment affects his behaviour and has noticed that his behaviour is less problematic if he is working in an environment that is structured and where instructions are given slowly, as he is then better able to manage the task. Padraig agrees, recognizing that he has difficulty comprehending what is asked of him when he is given too many instructions. However, his desire to keep pace with his peers escalates his anxiety and prevents him from attaining the calmness that his mother emphasizes as a key need.

A major problem for Padraig is the emphasis that is placed on his limitations. This creates anxieties for him and depresses his self-esteem. He desperately wants to fit in with his peers but, as we have noted, this desperation encourages him to behave in ways that are dysfunctional for him. He craves approval and positive reinforcement, but his belief that he works very well when he is interested or is stimulated is interpreted, by his teacher, as a lack of application to those things that do not interest him.

We can detect in Padraig's case many factors that, if exploited appropriately, could result in a very supportive environment for the boy, that could be socially, emotionally and educationally enriching. Padraig shows unusual insight into his own emotional need for positive reinforcement and recognition for his talents and achievements. He needs help, however, in managing what he experiences as pressure to conform to norms shared by his peers that are unsuited to his personal cognitive style. There is a role here for the teacher, with the support of the parent, to help Padraig develop the self-confidence to be different. This can be promoted by building Padraig's self-esteem, through acknowledgement of his high level of motivation to succeed and his positive achievements, and by helping him to identify the situations in which he copes most effectively with his concentration problems. However, working with Padraig in isolation from his peers is unlikely to be effective. In order for Padraig to overcome what he experiences as peer pressure to conform, a climate of tolerance for individual differences has to be established in the classroom and reflected in his parent's attitudes.

If we look at another example, we see the importance of utilizing resources outside the child's school and of forming partnerships.

Case study

Jacques' mother felt that she needed support in helping Jacques and was disappointed with the school's management of him and agreed for him to see someone from the family service unit (FSU), which involves one-to-one counselling and support for Jacques with a social worker. As she put it:

Parent: Well I joined the FSU at the beginning of the year, because I was really fed up; the school organized it for me. A social worker is helping Jacques, she says he sometimes gets fed up and doesn't really want to talk but sometimes he does. She takes him every Tuesday, for about an hour or so, then back to school.

Case study *continued*

There is a suggestion of a strong sense of empathy between the mother and son here, emphasized by the repeated use of the words 'fed up', indicating that both mother and son, according to the mother, have the same response to the difficulties they are encountering.

Significantly, Jacques' mother believes the support offered by the FSU has been beneficial for Jacques and thinks since going to the unit his behaviour at home is a lot calmer, but she remains unhappy with the school's continued negative attitude towards Jacques.

Parent: According to his teacher, 'Every time he's been to the FSU on a Tuesday; he comes back creating and carrying on'. But I think, 'Well there's only her who wants to really help'. But he's not too bad at home now, he's calming down. He has his off days and his good days, but I have my off days and good days.

Again, we see the empathy between mother and son – both have their 'off days and good days'. Her concern is that Jacques is not only misunderstood at school, but that there is a lack of support for him there. By contrast, Jacques's teacher sees the visits to the FSU unit as exacerbating what she sees as his attention-seeking behaviour in class:

Teacher: The thing is if you just leave him, and just let him get on with it, as long as he's not annoying the other children, then he will stop. It's attention-seeking basically.

She believes that this behaviour is best managed by ignoring him.

Jacques' view is different. The more people ignore him, the more upset and angry he becomes. From Jacques' point of view the withholding of attention seems to reinforce his feelings of low self-esteem and frustration:

Child: No one ever listens to me. Like mum, when I tell her a story she goes, 'Sshh', and tells me to shut up.

At first sight this reference to the mother's dismissal of the boy's storytelling may seem at odds with the empathic nature of the mother's attitude towards Jacques, noted above. However, this can also be interpreted as a reflection of the frustration that parents can sometimes feel when attempting to deal with what they see as a relentlessly demanding child. As the mother says (see above): 'He has his off days and his good days, but I have my off days and good days.' When their 'off days' occur at the same time, there is likely to be scope for this kind of conflict.

Jacques' story reveals another complex situation. In this case the mother blames the school for mismanaging her child. The teacher, however, sees Jacques as 'attention-seeking', and refuses to behave in ways that she believes will reinforce this behaviour. Furthermore, the teacher and parent have diametrically opposed views about the value of the support that Jacques receives from the FSU. The parent believes that Jacques benefits from the one-to-one support, whilst the teacher believes that this simply reinforces his attention-seeking tendencies. Jacques' perspective, however, encourages us to contrast the teacher's view with his own belief that he is often ignored and dismissed, thus making the FSU experience extremely valuable. There is a strong sense in this case study of enormous emotional stress in the family unit that is exacerbated by conflict with the school. The need for a non-judgemental dialogue to be opened is highly evident. This could be achieved through the teacher, the FSU and the parent getting together on a regular monthly basis to openly discuss the support given, and progress with Jacques' development.

Environment and medication

Children with ADHD can behave badly when they are taken out of a familiar environment.

Case study

Alan's mother has noticed that Alan's behaviour is better when he is occupied and when this is not possible his behaviour is disruptive, particularly when he is taken out of a familiar environment:

Parent: He is a total monster, if he was with other children, if he was occupied that way he wasn't too bad, but if he was bored he was just a nightmare.

In situations where Alan is away from his familiar environment his behaviour becomes restless and disruptive. Only when his attention is captured with some form of mental or physical activity does Alan's behaviour improve. Alan's teacher suggests that since commencing on medication Alan's academic work has improved:

Teacher: Academically he's doing more work and he's improving. In September, he wouldn't put pen to paper and couldn't be bothered, he will now and he'll do it willingly, and he wants to work, I mean he's still below the average, but he's far better than he was.

Alan's teacher explains that despite his medication enabling him to get on with his academic work, the way he is managed in class can make a difference to his behaviour. She has noticed that Alan is especially difficult to manage when his regular teacher is not on hand, such as when a supply teacher comes into class.

Both parent and teacher recognize that Alan's environment makes a difference to his behaviour and Alan, too, recognizes its importance. The teacher also notes that Alan benefits from predictable routines and structure, and requires constant reassurance. Alan states that he likes to work in quiet surroundings as noise distracts him making it difficult for him to concentrate, which leads him to distract others.

Once again, we get the sense that the child at the centre of this case is emotionally vulnerable. He is also seen by his mother as a serious source of concern and stress in the home. The teacher's attitude, however, seems positive, and there is an awareness, in both the home and school settings, of the kinds of circumstances that are most conducive to Alan's positive participation. There is evidence here, also, that efforts are being made to support Alan in both settings. The reference to medication, made by the teacher, suggests that it is seen as a positive intervention. In this case there appears to be a consensus among the key stakeholders, and an indication that the medical support is making a positive contribution. However, the effectiveness of medication can be increased by a couple of key actions:

■ Keep the child occupied with tasks that engage him, especially whilst he is under the influence of medication.

■ Avoid situations that challenge his emotions, especially changes in his environment such as a change in the curriculum or teaching staff.

Similarly, in this next example we can see the effectiveness of medication for improving concentration, and the importance of emotional calmness for reducing behavioural difficulties.

Case study

Sanjeev's mother struggles to find ways to manage Sanjeev's behaviour without using medication.

Parent: I just walk away and leave him to it, because no matter what you say to him, he'll just argue back with you when he's in that kind of a mood. He might have like this real tantrum, and then, 10 minutes later, he might come in, all calm again and say, 'I'm sorry'. And he's all right.

Sanjeev's mother is suggesting that the most effective way to diffuse a situation is to leave Sanjeev to calm down on his own. However, she has noticed that Ritalin is effective in enabling Sanjeev to concentrate when otherwise he would be restless.

Parent: We'd given him Ritalin on purpose, because the last time we were at the pantomime he just didn't concentrate and he didn't enjoy it. We thought we'll give him a tablet this time, see if he can concentrate better.

Sanjeev's mother has found Ritalin useful for helping Sanjeerv concentrate in class and in social situations. However, Sanjeev suggests that despite taking Ritalin he sometimes struggles with his work in class. He has experienced working in a group and working alone, and found the latter more productive.

Child: Once I just took ages to do a piece of work and then the teacher told me to go and sit on my own because I was being slow, and then I got my work done a lot faster, so I'd say I work better alone.

Sanjeev has found that without distractions he can focus on the task more easily and get his work done. However, he recognizes that although his concentration is better when working alone, he can become bored and unable to concentrate even with his favourite activities:

Child: I mean I've got the best computer what you can get, but I just get bored with it. In fact, say if I buy a game, after about a week I get really bored with it and then stop playing on it and then start playing on it again, and it just goes on and on. Then I leave it for about a couple of months and then I think, 'Oh, I remember that game, I haven't played on it for ages', so then I start playing it. But after another week I get bored with it, and then it just carries on.

Sanjeev has found that, when he becomes bored, he likes to find something more stimulating to do, and believes that everything becomes 'boring' after a while, but if left and then returned to at a later date his interest in it is renewed and he can resume the task. Sanjeev has identified his own way of relieving periods of 'boredom', he distracts himself from the task in hand and tries to keep his mind active on something else.

In this case, parent, teacher and child recognize that whilst medication can be useful, it is not a 'magic bullet'. They believe that medication can make Sanjeev restless, especially if he does not have a task to concentrate on. Sanjeev's teacher is aware that he receives medication to help him concentrate, but recognizes he still becomes distracted on some tasks, and is unsure as to why this remains a problem. Sanjeev prefers to work alone as he believes he can concentrate better, plus he recognizes that he likes his environment to be organized so that he knows what he is doing. Taken together, these various perspectives suggest that the positive effects of medication can be maximized by Sanjeev's parents and teacher working collaboratively to provide him with tasks that focus his thoughts, in an environment that is relatively-distraction free.

In this next example, the features of ADHD are perceived as positive characteristics, but providing tasks that maximize the child's concentration is the key to ensuring academic achievement.

Case study

Amy's teacher shows considerable insight when she states that she believes Amy's tendency to be overly talkative in class is not wilful, but rather is a feature of her particular brand of intelligence:

Teacher: I think that chattering and working at the same time is part of her intelligence. I keep her as busy as I can, so she can't go off. Because I think that's her problem a lot of the time, she just needs her mind to be active.

Keeping Amy stimulated in a focused and appropriate way has been an important factor in minimising the problems with her behaviour, both in class and in the home.

Amy recognizes that she has problems concentrating and remaining calm, and she believes that medication is helpful to her in this regard, but she also recognizes its limitations. An important feature of Amy's attitude to medication is that she sees it as a tool that she uses for her own purposes, rather than as something that is imposed on her for the benefit of others:

Child: I take tablets that calm me down when I need it, because after the four hours is nearly run out I feel giddy, but I calm down after I've taken it.

An important feature of this response is the child's willingness to take responsibility for her own behaviour, albeit through the use of medication. Clearly, however, Amy is attempting to manage her behaviour to enable herself to adapt to the classroom situation. Given her teacher's sympathetic and positive response to her need to 'chatter' whilst she works, it seems that there may be scope in this classroom for more accommodations to be made for Amy that might reduce the stress she experiences and make her less reliant on medication.

Practical classroom support for children with ADHD

A key message from these interviews, and other data sources in this study, is that the organizational structure of the classroom is influential in providing effective support for children with ADHD. Parents and teachers commonly identify the need for a structured environment, with clear guidance and instruction being an essential requirement of the support structure. Consistency is also recognized to be a major requirement, as is discipline and organization of routine. It is common for parents and children to suggest that school work needs to be done at the child's pace, rather than the pace being dictated by external drivers. There is also a recognition that children perform better when an adult scaffolds the work, enabling the child to recognize what is expected of him or her.

Teachers tend to emphasize that structure in the classroom situation provides children with the boundaries to guide their learning, and that working at the child's pace is also effective in producing work. Some teachers identify incidents where respecting the child's space or ways of working enabled more productive working. Teachers also tend to stress the importance of avoiding problem behaviour by steering children away from confrontational situations. Keeping the child calm is perceived by parents, teachers and children to be important not only for enabling productive work, but also for reducing the child's emotional outbursts. The importance of being respected and listened to is prominent in children's personal accounts. Children with ADHD commonly feel misunderstood, and there are several examples in this research of students complaining that they received insufficient appropriate attention of this kind. Although some parents and teachers suggested the use of medication for reducing hyperactivity and aiding concentration, some have found that encouraging monitored physical activity is a positive strategy to effectiveness.

Despite an overall awareness of effective and ineffective support for ADHD, there are many inconsistencies between children's, parents' and teachers' views, resulting in inappropriate or inconsistent support. An absence of consistency and coherence suggests a tendency among some parents, teachers and health and social care professionals to work in isolation from each other, rather than working together. In these circumstances the parent and child are often left with the job of trying to create coherence between the different professional inputs.

The need to work together

> The underlying philosophy for effective collaborative working is the ability for professions to have shared goals, to communicate with one another and to recognize and respect the roles and responsibilities of those they are working with.

Attention Deficit Hyperactivity Disorder is a multifactorial condition of which there is limited evidence of sustained improvement when support relies on provision from a single service provider. To achieve effective support for children with ADHD medical, educational and social services need to work together to ensure they provide co-ordinated services that meet the evolving needs of the child.

The role of a multidisciplinary approach for managing ADHD is supported by the National Institute for Clinical Excellence (NICE, 2002), which provides guidelines to the National Health Service (NHS) in England and Wales on the use of methylphenidate for this condition. It stipulates that methylphenidate should be used as part of a comprehensive treatment programme and that a diagnosis should be made only by clinicians who have expertise in ADHD and that the diagnosis should involve children, parents and carers and the child's school.

In addition, the guidelines suggest that once medication has commenced, regular monitoring needs to be maintained so that when the child's condition improves and is stable, treatment can be discontinued to determine whether further treatment is required. These guidelines target not only medication regimes, but call for prompt assessment and treatment and for improved interdisciplinary and interagency working, suggesting that health authorities and NHS Trusts work together with local authorities, social services and education to provide efficient services and appropriate provision (NICE, 2002).

This macro approach to childcare was endorsed in *Our Healthier Nation* (DoH, 1998), a document which prioritizes child health and highlights the need for improvements in the school environment as one means of achieving this priority. Whilst sensitive to the escalating numbers of children with special educational needs, the paper strongly advocates the need for these children to remain in mainstream schools. The paper describes good health being not only freedom from disease, but in terms of an individual's quality of life. It stipulates the need to consider social and economic, environmental and lifestyle factors as much as the genetic factors affecting health, and recognizes that poor mental health is damaging to physical health.

In the previous year, the government's Green Paper on education, *Excellence for All Children* (DfEE, 1997), prioritized the need for collaboration between agencies at local and national levels, supporting an integrated multidisciplinary approach by child health professionals, social services and education staff in the management of children who exhibit behavioural difficulties.

In assessing a child's needs, the government takes into account the importance of a child's emotional state. The 1993 Education Act states: 'the emotional development of children must continue to be a central concern for mainstream education' (DfEE, 1993: 16).

The Department for Education and Skills, in its attempt to ensure that children with special educational needs receive appropriate learning opportunities, identifies in the *Code of Practice* (DfES, 2001) six key principles:

- an emphasis on meeting pupil needs in mainstream provision, along with the recognition that alternative provision can play a role in a continuum of provision

- emphasis on ascertaining the views and wishes of the child in relation to SEN

- the importance of pupils having an entitlement and access to a broad, balanced and relevant curriculum

- the importance of partnership between parents and professionals and the central role of parents in supporting children's educational progress

- the important influence of complex and interacting factors in the educational setting on children's SEN

- the importance of early identification of SEN.

The document has particular relevance to children with ADHD as it refers to: 'children and young people who demonstrate features of emotional and behavioural difficulties, who are withdrawn or isolated, disruptive and disturbing, hyperactive and lack conversation; those with immature social skills; and those presenting challenging behaviours arising from other complex special needs' (DfES, 2001: 7.60).

In addition, the key principles identify the need for both parent and child to be involved in decision-making processes, and for parents to have their perspectives on what is required in way of support for them and their child considered by professionals. The document refers to the collaboration of service provision by stating that: 'consultation and open discussion with the child's parents, the school doctor or the child's general practitioner, the community paediatrician and any specialist services providing treatment for the child will be essential to ensure that the child makes maximum progress' (DfES, 2001: 7.60).

Such collaboration should also ensure that the child is not unnecessarily excluded from any part of the curriculum or school activity because of anxiety about his or her care and treatment. This statement is an example of how service providers can co-ordinate their services to ensure that provision is directly secured around the evolving needs of the child and that they are not in danger of receiving unco-ordinated or inconsistent support. If all members of the child's support network are familiar with the decision and management structure in place, and equally aware of any changes, they are better placed to be able to meet the child's needs.

As part of the strategy for collaboration between the professions, the Code of Practice (DfES, 2001) suggests that parents of children with special educational needs should be empowered to work with the schools and local services. Uniting agencies in this way removes the mystification surrounding educational and health services. This multidisciplinary approach is echoed in *Every Child Matters* (DfES, 2004), which stipulates that for its aim's to be met, organizations involved with providing services to children will need to team up in new ways, sharing information and working together. The document makes reference to children and young people having more say about issues that affect them, and that local authorities will need to work with their respective partners to find out what works best for children in order to deliver appropriate services, and that the children themselves will be involved in this process.

However, despite policy guidelines advocating a collaborative approach, these guidelines are often vague about the reality of how this might happen. Services tend to have separate management policies, budget planning and organizational structures, as well as uni-professional guidelines. It should be stated that efforts are being made by the UK government to overcome philosophical and operational difficulties created by such compartmentalization through the development of integrated children's services. At the time of writing it is not clear that the long-standing barriers to such integration have as yet been overcome successfully.

Involving the child in collaborative working

The call for collaboration of services is further endorsed through the 1989 Children Act, which has at the centre of its policy the need for the child's voice to be heard. There is recognition that children need to be involved in decisions that will affect them, especially in the area of special educational needs. In reference to the child, the legislation states that: 'children have a point of view and must be consulted about decisions which affect them … their support is crucial to the effective implementation of any individual education programme' (DfEE, 1989: 2.34–2.36).

These guidelines are supported in the SEN *Code of Practice* which stresses the importance of partnership between the teacher and the pupil. It advocates that children be fully involved in the 'dialogue' of learning, and in the decision-making and disciplinary process (DfES, 2001).

The emphasis is not only on learning, but on the child developing a positive sense of self. The government's Green Paper, *Excellence for All Children* (DfEE, 1997), proposed that, from September 1998, schools were to assess all children at the beginning of their primary education to identify where they may need help, and local authorities were highlighted as being responsible for providing support and resources to meet the local educational needs of children. The document favours schools collaborating with parents, and other agencies (especially educational psychologists), in achieving the quest to support children's needs. It recognizes that parents may need support from both the statutory and voluntary services, and supports the need for training for teachers to strengthen their skills in managing behavioural problems in the classroom.

The strong emphasis on the importance of participation of parents and children in the assessment processes represents a very important step forward in government thinking about the need for professionals, parents and children to work together for the benefit of the child. However, Armstrong et al. (1993) suggest that there is a lack of evidence that children's needs are being addressed in social and educational policy. They argue that the child's needs are still being defined predominantly from the professionals' perspective. They further argue that professionals are giving 'lip service' to involving the child in the decision-making. They conclude that professionals lack appropriate skills to listen to children, or to identify with their needs. These authors advocate that the most appropriate way for professionals to assess the needs of a child is for them to acknowledge the child's own perceptions and meanings, rather than to draw implications from observing the child's behaviour or from the interpretation of others.

Unfortunately, the present study shows little evidence of active, constructive dialogue taking place between professionals and parents or children. The professionals, in the examples we have explored, are the key decision-makers within their professional domains, and the children and parents are very conscious of being outside the decision-making processes, often to their frustration. This is not to say that professionals do not sometimes make appropriate decisions and take actions that benefit the child and parents. It is clear, however, as we have noted repeatedly, that opportunities that might emerge from constructive dialogue to understand the child's circumstances and needs more fully are often not taken. This study therefore supports the findings of Armstrong el al. (1993), that the legislative and advisory rhetoric on parent and child participation is not observable in practice.

The importance of listening to children cannot be underestimated: if a comprehensive programme is to be developed for managing children with ADHD, then they need to be involved in the decision-making. Bennathan and Boxall (2003) suggest that a child's experience of life is the reality that needs to be captured and that listening to children provides them with the opportunity to: 'form a concept of themselves from the way they have been treated and through this they assess what is happening to them' (Bennathan and Boxall, 2003: 105). They highlight the importance of understanding behaviour from the perspective of the person behind the behaviour and report that 'most behaviour … makes sense if seen through the eyes of the behaver' (Bennathan and Boxall, 2003: 106).

This suggests that it is the meaning of behaviour that is captured when a child explains their actions, and that misinterpreted behaviour may give rise to a child developing a negative concept about adults who have misinterpreted their behaviour. Bennathan and Boxall (2003) warn that children who have experienced early negative concepts of adults may carry these with them into school and the wider world, and generalize negative concepts towards all adults unless taught otherwise by those responsible for their development. They suggest that children's feelings about events or situations need to be understood in order for support to be provided. In other words, negative concepts from adults may influence and exacerbate negative behaviour in children, behaviour that they may carry with them into adulthood. Therefore, if health and education services are to support children with ADHD, the child's perspective about their difficulties needs to be understood (Hughes, 2004).

Evidence of collaborative working

Collaborative working is endorsed by policy guidelines, but the availability of guidelines about how education, health and social services can work together, or how their respective organizational structure can best support collaborative working is limited. As it happens, ADHD is one of the few areas where there are, albeit brief, guidelines for multidisciplinary working (BPS, 2000).

One the challenges to the development of multidisciplinary working resides in the fact that professionals are generally trained to understand the needs of the service user from the perspective of their professional discipline. They are trained to be competent in the process of assessing and managing the needs of service users from their professional orientation of conduct and practice. This includes professional confidentiality and decision-making, and given that medical professionals are trained to diagnose and treat health problems, and teachers are trained to deliver curriculum, they have different objectives. The result is that when they are involved in delivering services for a multifactorial condition like ADHD, they have competing professional, political and economic agendas (Galloway, 2001; Timimi, 2002).

In the 1990s, service providers at the forefront of delivering collaborative provision were becoming aware of the difficulties of bringing together professions from other disciplines. Appleton et al. (1997) report on a study around the care of 21 children, all of whom had complex and severe impairments and had been referred to the health and education services for consideration for educational statementing. Care co-ordinators were involved in the team to provide a structured assessment plan focusing on each family's and child's needs, and were responsible for preparing a care plan for home and school, and for co-ordinating case reviews. Initial findings from the study provide evidence of effective teamworking. In particular, the findings report that parents were satisfied with having a named co-ordinator to whom they could address issues that could then be referred on to the appropriate service. However, despite these initial positive findings, the study identified the need for flexible and well-resourced administrative structures that could support the children's evolving needs. In other words, initial collaborative working cannot be sustained as teamwork requires more than just policy guidelines to develop and sustain collaboration.

Guzzo and Shea (1992) propose that for effective teamwork individuals need to feel they are important to the success of the team. Each team member's role should be meaningful and intrinsically rewarding and individual contributions should be identifiable and subject to evaluation. In addition, West and Poulton (1997) emphasize that it is not only essential to create a team structure; they also advise that teamwork will only be possible if clear objectives guide the work activities and co-ordination amongst the team members.

As a guide to agencies preparing to develop collaborative programmes, West and Poulton (1997) suggest four significant indicators:

- Aims, goals and objectives are agreed.

- There is effective communication.

- Patients receive the best possible care.

- Individual roles are defined and understood.

However, whilst a group's internal process is important for effectiveness, organizational boundaries need to be identified. Field and West (1995) suggest that individual professional groups not only need a clear understanding of their own role in the team, but also a well-defined appreciation of other members' roles and contribution to patient care. Miller et al. (1999) report on a three-year study commissioned in 1996 by the English National Board for Nursing, Midwifery and Health Visiting which looked into existing multi-professional working within clinical practice. Miller et al. (1999) identified that differing perceptions of what it is to be a member of a multi-professional group had a negative impact on the way the team functioned. In particular different perceptions caused:

- a mismatch of team awareness

- a mismatch of role expectations

- a mismatch of communication expectations.

'The mismatch led to conflict and resentment. Holding different conceptualisations of multi-professional teamwork led to deleterious outcomes in terms of both professional interaction and, apparently, patient care' (Miller et al., 1999: 96).

However, the report found that in teams where there was effective collaborative working 'there were clear benefits for patients, carers and the team itself' (Miller et al. 1999: 219), including continuity and consistency of care, a reduction in ambiguous messages between team members and clients, and appropriate referral procedures in terms of profession and timing. The clear evidence of the benefits of effective collaborative working for members and clients demonstrates that, despite difficulties in achieving success, collaborative working improves service provision.

Making collaborative working work in your school

Children with ADHD have diverse needs, which are fragmented and evolving, and therefore require support from more than one service provider. However, collaborative working is not merely about co-ordinating services, but also maintaining them, especially when the demand is for long-term support across professions. Øvretveit (1993) suggests it is the balance of resources that dictates co-ordination. He suggests that that when the needs of a client are complex and cross professional services, it is the team players that need their services co-ordinated in order to ensure they deliver effectively and avoid any duplication of skills. In providing a co-ordinated service for a child with ADHD, sustaining the services needs to be taken into account as these will change along with the evolving needs of the child. Attempting to co-ordinate service provision for children is not a new concept: child development teams led by doctors have been used to centralize resources (Bax and Whitmore, 1991). However, the changing needs of children and their families prompted some teams to direct the leadership to another profession (Yerbury, 1997).

One of the major concerns for any team is one of organization and accountability. For example, a team member may belong to the team but professionally be accountable to another line manager; the demands and constraints are therefore prioritized between profession and team. Yerbury (1997), reporting from care co-ordination teams in Canada, argues that in situations where the team manager is the key player and the only line manager holding a budget for health services, social and educational services and charitable organizations, then no such conflict arises.

An example of autonomy within a team is the community mental health teams (CMHT). These have autonomy to manage their own budgets, and as a consequence are flexible to respond to the needs of the client whilst working within their financial constraints. Budget holding therefore may be the key to enabling child healthcare teams to co-ordinate their services and provide the training and support needed for staff. However, this does not remove the difficulties of a multidisciplinary team whose responsibilities and professional status lie with services outside the team.

Hall (1997) suggests an '**empowerment** model' where the team focuses on the children and their families so as to respond to their evolving requirements. Hall suggests it is the role of the professions to provide parents with the information they need in order to direct these requirements. This empowerment model includes parents in partnership with professionals in assessment, decision-making and evaluation of services, and suggests that decisions to provide a service should not be guided by financial cost and length of time; rather they should be guided by what is in the best interest of the child.

As a means of including parents, carers and children in the assessment and intervention procedures, the British Psychological Society (BPS) recommends that non-technical vocabulary is used so that understanding is made easier and cultural factors are taken into account to ensure that procedures for assessment and intervention do not discriminate against minority subgroups (BPS, 1996; 2000).

Suggestions of what to do in your school

- Work in partnership to include stakeholders, parent(s) and child.
- Place the needs of the child at the centre of negotiations.
- Clarify team organization, responsibility and accountability.
- Develop a strategy that addresses the co-ordination and distribution of services/resources/skills.
- Identify a tool to monitor behaviour change.

Despite the controversy over what constitutes an effective multidisciplinary team and what should be provided in terms of provision, it is clear that organizational constraints and the political and professional focus of the players need to be addressed if parental partnership is to be included, and for teams to provide a flexible evolving service. However, despite the discussion being about children with disabilities, it has not been made explicit how partnerships may invite children to identify their needs. Therefore, although parental rights are recognized, children's rights are not. Kelly's suggestion, of seeking clarity by asking the person to explain their difficulties to you, seems a good starting point (Kelly, 1955).

The consequence of perceiving a condition as complex as ADHD, through a single professional lens, is the danger that the condition is construed in a manner that is at odds with the ways in which other professionals may view it. Furthermore, the closed world of the professional discipline not only creates barriers to understanding among members of other disciplines, but it also places the non-professional in a situation where he or she may have difficulty understanding any of the various professional discourses. This situation is not conducive to effective communication between professionals and between professionals and clients. This, in turn, hampers the processes of identification, assessment and intervention. Therefore, although current policy documents stimulate the need for collaborative working, they fail to provide professionals and organizations with the required tools to ensure this happens.

Collaborative working, that embraces professional, parental and child perspectives, requires co-operation and commitment, but it also requires a framework which will facilitate this. The next chapter explores potential models for collaborative working.

Key points to remember

- ◆ Work in partnership with the stakeholders and develop a strategy for organizing and co-ordinating resources and dialogue.

- ◆ Place the child's needs at the centre of negotiations, listen to the child and involve him or her in the decision-making.

- ◆ Avoid emphasizing the child's limitations by supporting his or her discreetly as you reinforce their strengths.

- ◆ Maintain the child's quest for a stimulated environment through tasks that require his or her concentration.

- ◆ Provide a learning environment that does not challenge the child's emotions or distract his or her concentration.

Models for Collaborative Working

This chapter attempts to identify a framework for achieving collaborative working across professional boundaries by exploring different theoretical models and relating some of these to a single case scenario of a child with ADHD. The models described below can be used individually or combined with one another. However, the key factor is that they represent a framework for achieving not only collaborative working, but appropriate bio-psychosocial support for children with ADHD.

- ◆ Why use a framework?
- ◆ Problem-based model
  - Eight-stage model
- ◆ The Leicester model of inter-professional education
- ◆ A bio-psychosocial model
- ◆ The systematic analysis model
- ◆ Example of utilizing the models
  - Application of an action plan to support a child's behaviour
- ◆ What next?
  - A few words of caution
- ◆ Key points to remember

Why use a framework?

Attention Deficit Hyperactivity Disorder is a condition that affects all areas of a child's development. Therefore it is the long-term reduction of symptoms, coupled with interventions designed to support active, positive development, that are necessary to enable the child to reach their normal developmental milestones. If ADHD is to be recognized as a bio-psychosocial condition, then the assessment, the decision-making about the required support, and the evaluation of its effectiveness must reflect this. To provide and sustain such a framework, professionals and parents need to work together, diligently, and in line with the child's changing social, emotional and academic needs.

The British Psychological Society, in its guidelines for multidiscipilinary working for children with ADHD, strongly endorses the view that: 'consultation between agencies, disciplines and professionals should take place in order to disseminate information on the roles and practices of the different groups' (BPS, 2000: 7). The guidelines conclude that, 'shared knowledge and understanding of each other's practice and roles is essential to understand the complex nature of ADHD' (BPS 2000: 7), and that parents and children are part of the shared focus in the multi-professional organization of care.

Working collaboratively cannot be achieved through legislation alone; the call for a collaborative workforce, where professional boundaries are broken, depends on professionals being willing and able to collaborate with others. In addition to a will to work together there needs to be a shared purpose across professional and organizational domains. In the case of children with ADHD the common purpose for doctors, teachers, parents and the child is to improve the child's behaviour and promote positive, social, emotional and academic development and functioning. These shared purposes can act as a web to capture the knowledge and skills of professions, and thereby form the framework for supporting the child with ADHD.

The processes by which professionals exchange information and create the web are an important factor in the success of collaborative working. Problem-based learning (PBL) is one such process that lends itself to capturing the knowledge and skills of different professions, enabling reflection and analysis to inform decision-making and change (Hughes and Lucas, 1997). If used appropriately, this process can act as a tool to create the web of information needed to support children with ADHD and as the means by which professionals, parents and children can work together.

Problem-based model

A problem-based approach engages individuals in the exchange of information and encourages both reflection on knowledge and a search for a greater understanding of issues. For example, you might know that a child can display disruptive behaviour in class, but you do not know why this behaviour varies between classes or between teachers. When we are faced with a child who is diagnosed with ADHD and whose behaviour is problematic we make on-the-spot decisions, many of which are based on personal perspectives about the child and incidents at that time. Rarely are we asked to describe how we arrived at our decision and rarely do we know about or have an understanding of the different approaches used by others or the effectiveness of these approaches.

The key to effective problem-based learning is the definition of the problem. In the case of ADHD, it is common for the a child's difficulties to be defined in terms of learning and/or behavioural difficulties. In the group situation, with, for example, the class teachers, special educational needs specialists and a child's parents, the problem-based learning process enables them to discover what is already known, and what needs to be known in order to understand the child within the situations in which the problems arise. Sharing knowledge in the group provides a horizontal collection of information that is pertinent to the problem (Woods, 1994) and gives a greater understanding not only of the problem across settings, but of how best to provide consistent support. When a group made up of different disciplines comes together to explore the complexities of a child with ADHD, the process of a problem-based approach encourages a lateral perspective to problem-solving enabling a rich mix of knowledge, skills and experiences to be rigorously explored.

Problem-based learning is used in many universities across a number of disciplines. More recently it has been used to facilitate inter-professional learning and to encourage collaborative practice (Hughes and Lucas, 1997). The problem-based learning process varies within institutions, but for the purpose of this chapter we use a systematic 'eight-stage' approach (see Figure 6.1). The stages guide the process and engage members, but it is important that all group members are involved in each stage of the process and that the stages become the cornerstone by which to manage evolving issues. As problems and issues are identified, this increases understanding and directs further inquiry and decision-making within the group.

Figure 6.1 The eight-stage problem-based model (adapted from Burrows and Tamblyn, 1980)

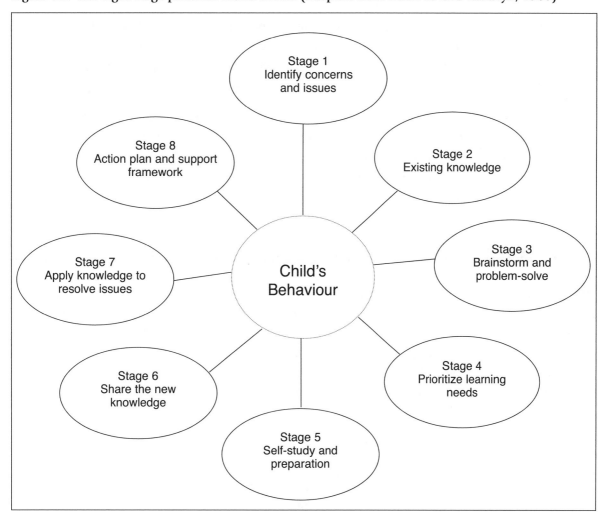

Stage 1: Identify concerns Group members briefly identify each concern/issue as an individual item.

Stage 2: Existing knowledge Consider each concern/issue with your existing knowledge. This will enable you to clarify what you know already, and what others know about the concerns.

Stage 3: Problem-solve Brainstorm the concerns/issues to identify what you <u>do not know</u> and therefore what you <u>need to know</u> to resolve the problems. This creates many new ideas, some may overlap but ultimately major categories will emerge.

Stage 4: Prioritize learning needs The categories will need to be prioritized for further exploration and understanding. The group needs to agree on learning goals and objectives to allocate work and resources.

Stage 5: Self-study and preparation Greater understanding and clarification of issues can be achieved by individual members or as a whole group.

Stage 6: Share the new knowledge New knowledge should be shared with the group so that all members learn from one another.

Stage 7: Apply the knowledge to resolve the issues Applying the new knowledge provides greater insight to the original issues, enabling them to be viewed in a new light. The group is then better able to identify the skills and competencies needed to tackle the issues and to allocate tasks to the most appropriate person(s).

Stage 8: Action plan Develop an action plan to support your new approach to resolve the issues. Agree on how you will organize, deliver and co-ordinate the information, services and support, and how you will involve others/services outside your group/organization. Identify clear routes of communication and develop a strategy to monitor effectiveness of change.

The Leicester model of inter-professional education

The Leicester model of inter-professional education (Anderson et al., 2003) (Figure 6.2), is another problem-based approach, used in the education curriculum for health and social care workers to encourage collaborative working in practice. The model has been adapted for this chapter to show how it can be applied not only to encourage interdisciplinary working to support a child with ADHD, but how professionals can achieve a support structure that is consistent with the child's perception of requirements. In the model, professions are encouraged to draw on the child's knowledge to inform the decision-making process for change.

Figure 6.2 The Leicester Model (adapted from Anderson et al., 2003)

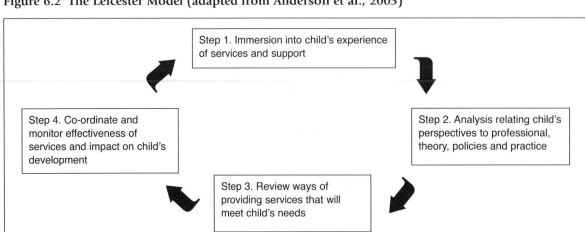

Step 1 Professionals individually talk with the child to gain his or her perspective on his or her own behaviour in both the home and school setting, with a view to understanding the impact on the child's physical, psychological and social functioning. The child's priorities and attitudes are explored alongside their relationship with the services and support they receive

Step 2 The professionals come together to discuss the child's perspectives and how these relate to the understanding, roles and the services they offer. The child's perspective is debated and the strengths and deficiencies of service support identified.

Step 3 The professional group is now able to theorize over how best to provide services and support that directly impact on the needs of the child, and how to draw on other service provision if required.

Step 4 The education cycle is completed with group members co-ordinating and evaluating the effectiveness of support services by monitoring the child's development and behaviour, and revisiting Step 1 to assess achievement and change, and the impact on the child's perspective.

The problem-based models (Figures 6.1 and 6.2) serve to identify a process for professionals, parents and the child to use in identifying and resolving concerns/issues. However, bearing in mind the complexity of ADHD, we suggest two other models that are useful in conjunction with the above models: the bio-psychosocial model and the systematic analysis model.

A bio-psychosocial model

A bio-psychosocial model (Figure 6.3) (based on Cooper, 2006) provides a framework from which teachers and parents can explore the child's behaviour by considering how bio-psychological and social factors may be contributing to the child's difficulties. The model is appropriate to use at Stages 2 and 8 of the problem-based model (Figure 6.1) as it enables you to consider the thought processes behind the issues raised and those that are raised by others. This model can also be used to monitor the effectiveness of intervention and support strategies as it enables you to consider the interplay among biological, psychological and social factors, and its effect on behaviour.

This bio-psychosocial model attempts to capture the complex interplay of biological, social and psychological factors in a given 'problem' situation, and match these factors to possible interventions. By plotting the ways in which different factors involved in the situation fall into one or more of the six cells dealing with the 'manifestation of problems' (Figure 6.3), the problem-solvers can begin to identify possible avenues for intervention, drawing on different knowledge sources. Often, of course, the particular issues identified will not always fall discretely into a single cell, but will overlap across two or more cells. The model captures systematically each main concern for example, disruptive behaviour, inattentiveness, social problems or anxiety and enables to be considered repeatedly bio-psychosocial dimensions across different settings. For example, the model could be used in the classroom for each lesson or subject, or compared with the perspectives of teacher(s) and parent(s). A more simplified version could be used by the child to ensure his or her perspective is obtained for both the home and school setting.

Figure 6.3 A Bio-psychosocial Model (Based on Cooper, 2006)

IDENTIFICATION ASSESSMENT AND INTERVENTION	Manifestation of problems	Biological	Psychological	Social
	INTERNAL To the child			
	EXTERNAL To the child			
		Biological	Psychological	Social

The systemic analysis (progressive focusing) model

The systematic analysis, or progressive focussing model (Figure 6.4) (Cooper, 2006) involves systematically reflecting on the impact the six factors have on the child's functioning, beginning with the factor that is most removed from the child's personality. For example, you begin by considering how the child functions in the curriculum, then how he or she functions in his or her physical, then institutional, environment, before considering how he or she functions in his or her social environment and then with his or her pupil group, before finally considering how the child functions as an individual.

Figure 6.4 The systematic analysis (progressive focusing) model (based on Cooper, 2006)

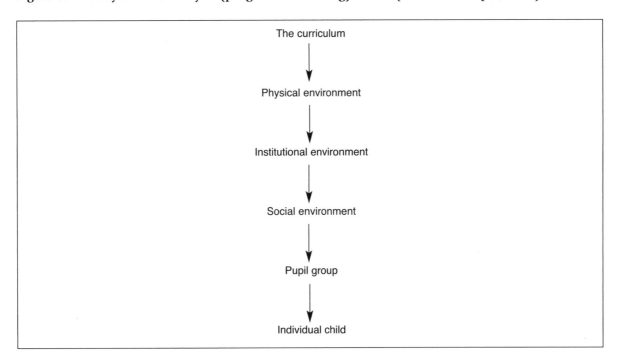

The purpose of considering each factor or theme in isolation before progressing on to the next is that it avoids making immediate assumptions about a particular problem being perceived as relating only to the child. In addition, the process of analysing each factor or theme in conjunction with the bio-psychosocial model provides teachers with a wider framework from which to reflect on behaviour. The reflection process and the knowledge gained from this exercise complement Stages 3 and 8 of the eight-stage process in the problem-based model.

These two models (Figures 6.3 and 6.4), when used in conjunction with one of the problem-based models, provide a framework for considering the child's behaviour in a number of contexts. When the framework is used with members from a range of disciplines comprising parents, teachers, psychologists and support teachers, we are able to consider the child's behaviour across a number of contexts rather than in isolation. This provides teachers with knowledge about the similarities and differences in behaviour and the impact environmental and organizational factors have on behaviour. This knowledge, along with an increased understanding of the efficacy of intervention strategies, provide a greater understanding of the roles of colleagues and enable stakeholders to be more proficient in providing support for the child.

Example of utilizing the models

The models described above can be used in isolation or together, and can be adapted to meet the needs of the child's behaviour and the concerns of teachers, parents and other professionals. The following scenario serves as a guide on how the models can support a child with ADHD.

Scenario

The teacher is concerned about Mark, a child who although generally perceived to be 'bright' in terms of his verbal responses is persistently disruptive in class. In addition to disruptive outbursts he is failing to do his work, despite repeated instructions. He becomes aggressive towards some teachers and peers for no apparent reason, and being reprimanded seems to aggravate the situation. The teacher is concerned that despite Mark being recently prescribed Ritalin as a result of being diagnosed as having ADHD, the child's behaviour is deteriorating.

In this type of situation the teacher, headteacher, support teacher and the child's parents need to work together to identify concerns, share knowledge and find an agreed approach to support the child. When the group meets, they will find the models useful for providing a framework to explore concerns and knowledge, and for enabling the group to learn to work together in developing a shared understanding to provide support for themselves and the child.

Application of an action plan to support a child's behaviour

Stage 1: Identify concerns and issues The group review the child's behaviour and create an hypothesis for each aspect of concern. For example, 'Unless the child has his medication his behaviour is disruptive', 'In literacy sessions the child always behaves in a disruptive manner', 'In sport sessions the child is aggressive with his peers and the teacher' or 'At home the child does not like to play with other children'. The concerns are formed into four hypotheses which the group can now explore in more detail.

Stage 2: Explore existing knowledge The group explores each hypothesis, one at a time, and uses the bio-psychosocial model to provide a macro perspective on the concerns. The model helps the group to consider whether they perceive the child's behaviour is as the consequence of internal or external factors. For example, the child may be described by teachers as being disruptive and therefore this behaviour is perceived to be caused by the child. However, the support teacher and parent may identify that the child's disruptive behaviour occurs when many instructions are given to the child. The latter suggests that the source of the disruptive behaviour may be external to the child and resides within the psychological domain.

The process of analysing concerns enables the group to explore them in detail, identifying what they already know about each hypothesis and listening to the perspectives and concerns held by other group members. It is at this stage that the child's positive attributes can also be explored, because they could serve as an example as to which factors exacerbate positive behaviour.

Stage 3: Brainstorm and problem-solve This stage of the process enables the group to consider what they do not know about the concerns they have just raised. This process is aided by the systematic analysis model, which identifies six themes for the group to consider as they debate each hypothesis and begin to formulate gaps in their knowledge. For example, in considering the role of medication the group may recognize its benefit as being to prevent disruptive behaviour. As the group explores the child's behaviour in relation to each theme, they will begin to find areas that they need to understand more fully. They may find that in certain situations disruptive behaviour is not a concern, that with some teachers disruptive behaviour does not occur at all or that it is only disruptive under certain conditions. The group may find that their differing perspectives require them to gain a greater understanding about the role of medication and teaching styles. Gaps in the group's knowledge about a situation or concern identify the areas that need to be explored further and the learning needs for the next stage.

Stage 4: Prioritize learning needs In a group situation the gaps in knowledge can either be explored in full by each member of the group or distributed equally across the group, giving each member the responsibility of pursuing one area/project.

Stage 5: Self-study and preparation Develop a greater depth of knowledge about concerns and issues related to the child's behaviour so that you can use this information to re-evaluate the way you think about the issues, and inform others about your broader view.

Stage 6: Share new knowledge The group meets to share the new knowledge and to ensure they all understand and agree with what has been found. This stage ensures that they are aware of the work their colleagues have been involved with and allows for misunderstandings to be addressed, thereby preparing them for the next stage. For example, they should have a clear understanding of how medication works and the implications of the child's learning environment on the effectiveness of medication.

Stage 7: Apply the knowledge to resolve issues This stage requires the group to reflect on the original concerns and to reappraise these in light of their new knowledge. The group is now in a better position to identify the skills and competencies needed to address any changes required in the child's behaviour.

Stage 8: Action plan and support framework The group needs to identify how they are going to implement the appropriate changes to address their original hypothesis. The new knowledge will have changed the group's perspectives and provided them with a greater understanding of the roles of the other members. Using the bio-psychosocial model, and the systematic analysis model, tasks and processes can be directed to the most appropriate person(s). Consistency and co-ordination of action can be monitored through further group meetings as change in the child's behaviour is reported and the support framework is altered accordingly.

What next?

By the end of the eight-stage process the group should be clear about the following:

- what the 'real' concerns are

- the child's perspective

- where support is required

- the order of priority for support

- who is doing what

- the timescale

- a strategy for monitoring effectiveness of support

- a strategy for managing the child's revolving needs.

A few words of caution

One of the dangers with identifying 'concerns/issues' is that we may run the risk of pathologizing the individual child, that is, tending to see him or her solely in terms of difficulties. This can be harmful to the child, not least because it may lead to the child's positive qualities becoming blurred. Research suggests that children with ADHD have many positive qualities (Cooper and Shea, 1997; Hughes, 2004). As one explores the problems relating to the child with ADHD it is important also to explore the child's positive qualities; that is, the things that he or she does well and the strengths that he or she has (see Cooper and Bilton, 2002). These positive qualities need to be further developed and form part of the objectives in the support framework.

Key questions to be asked are always:

- What does he or she do well?

- In what circumstances do these positives occur?

- What can be done to increase the frequency with which he or she inhabits these positive circumstances and experiences the rewards of doing things well?

We have purposely identified in-built features in the models presented in this chapter that seek to avoid assuming that concerns/issues are automatically located within the child. This is a conscious effort on behalf of the authors to portray to readers that identifying positives will aid the processes of problem identification and the devising of well-reasoned interventions.

Key points to remember

◆ Working together requires professions and parents to communicate and identify a shared purpose and vision for children.

◆ A problems based approach establishes a focus for engaging and exchanging information.

◆ The child's evolving needs can be identified by one or more of the suggested models which will enable agencies to monitor the effectiveness of intervention and support.

◆ When exploring the needs of the child with ADHD it is important to identify and clarify their positive achievements and traits.

CHAPTER 7

Educational Interventions for ADHD

In this chapter, we focus entirely on educational interventions for ADHD.

- ◆ How is effective teaching learned?
- ◆ What do we know about how teachers think?
  - – How do teachers think?
  - – How teachers think about pupils
- ◆ Effective learning and teaching episodes
- ◆ Teachers' knowledge of effective pedagogy
- ◆ How to make your teaching style work for pupils with ADHD
  - – Cognitive strategies
- ◆ Educational strategies for managing the learning context for pupils with ADHD
- ◆ ADHD and nurture groups
- ◆ Key points to remember

There are several reasons for focusing on educational interventions for ADHD. First, given that ADHD is still largely seen as a problem affecting school-aged children, and is indeed defined in terms that suggest that it is in schools that ADHD is often first noticed because of its disruptive effect on the educational progress of the pupil and his or her peers, it is surprising that most of the published research on ADHD focuses on its medical and neuropsychological aspects. There is relatively less research on effective teaching for pupils with ADHD, though there is very useful evidence as to what makes for effective educational intervention for ADHD. This might be taken to suggest that there is an imbalance in the way in which ADHD is portrayed in the academic and professional literature on the topic. This chapter sets out to redress this imbalance.

Second, although teachers, and other adults in schools, might rightly see themselves as representing only one element in the ADHD intervention process, they are definitely in the 'front line' in relation to this issue. After parents, teachers are the people most of us spend most of our time with between the ages of 5 and 16. It is vital, therefore, that teachers develop an understanding of how best to deal with ADHD, which, on average, affects one or two children in every class of 30, and far more than this in many classrooms – especially those comprising of largely lower-attaining pupils or those who are perceived to be behaviourally challenging.

Third, it is argued that an understanding of ADHD, and appropriate educational responses to it, leads to teaching strategies that benefit pupils far beyond the range of those who are diagnosed, or who could be diagnosed, with ADHD. After all, students exhibiting attentional problems are a key challenge for teachers of all kinds, from kindergarten classrooms, to teachers' conferences, to doctoral seminars and beyond. Only some of these might qualify for the diagnosis of ADHD.

Fourth, there is research evidence to suggest that there are important aspects of the ways in which experienced teachers tend to think and act that appear to make the ADHD concept particularly useful for pedagogical purposes. This chapter develops this idea, first, through an account of what we mean by 'pedagogy' and, then, through an analysis of how teachers might incorporate knowledge of ADHD into their pedagogical thinking.

How is effective teaching learned?

Effective teaching is not simply something that can be learned from a manual of strategies. In the case of ADHD, simply knowing the kinds of strategies that some teachers have used successfully will not be enough to equip them with the skills they need. Because successful teaching is such a complex activity, it is always necessary for teachers to be able to make decisions on the basis of their *understanding* of what is required, pedagogically, in a specific situation. The quick and decisive thinking that characterizes effective teaching is always rooted in the experience and knowledge of the teacher. This is an obvious point to anyone who has observed (or experienced) differences in the performance of novice and expert practitioners in any area of professional practice. For example:

> The novice teacher may imitate the behaviours of their expert mentor in the way in which they introduce a particular learning experience to a group of students, but achieve quite different results. The expert teacher, established in the school and well known to the class, might instruct the students to 'choose someone you know, and make a list of the reasons why you might recommend, or not recommend the TV programme, that the whole-class has seen, to that person'. In the expert teacher's classroom, this stimulates a whole-class exploration of issues of 'audience', which involves different students engaging with the topic in different, but complementary ways. When the novice teacher tries the same approach, the result is completely different. The initial reaction from some students will challenge the validity of the task ('Why are we doing this?'); others will subvert it ('That programme was just crap – that's my list!'); others might simply ignore the instruction and engage in off-task behaviour; those who engage as they might for the expert teacher are vilified by others in the class ('Leave it to the boffs'). The novice teacher confronted with these circumstances might believe he or she has failed, only to be told by the 'expert' that he or she had exactly the same experience when he or she first tried the same strategy. 'There are,' the mentor explains, 'quite a few other things to sort out before you can do that sort of thing with 8X. This is how I got to that point … '. Of course, other 'mentors' might comment that: 'Well, that doesn't happen when *I* do that very same activity with 8X. Are you sure you are cut out for this job?'

This anecdote suggests that there is more than one way to achieve a desired performance. Or, to put it another way, the thought processes involved in producing apparently similar performance may be quite different from teacher to teacher. It is insights such as these that gave rise to a now established way of thinking about teaching as being analogous to a 'craft'.

What do we know about how teachers think?

How do teachers think?

Not everyone is comfortable with the idea that teaching can be construed as a 'craft'. It is clearly a source of dismay to some educational academics that the practice of teaching is not easily influenced by their theorizing. One president of the American Educational Research Association (AERA), in her presidential address to the annual AERA conference, complained that: 'School practices are influenced by outmoded theories of learning and development that are relics of psychology's behaviorist past … Contemporary theories are making little headway in influencing school practices' (Brown and McIntyre, 1993, quoted in Monro, 1999: 11).

In the field of special education this view is reflected in the writings of those who challenge what they see as some teachers' unwitting collusion in the social exclusion of students who are disadvantaged by the application of pathological labels such ADHD (see for example, Booth and Ainscow, 1998; Slee, 1995). These writers portray many teachers as operating with outmoded theories (such as an often ill-defined 'medical model') that fail to take account of theories that emphasize ways in which social and institutional factors can serve to construct 'disabilities' and 'special needs'. For example:

> When a teacher, perceiving the child with ADHD as having a biological dysfunction because they have been prescribed psycho-stimulant medication, adopts the understanding that medication will 'normalize' the child's behaviour, taking this theoretical stance ignores the psychological and social factors impacting on the child and excludes the relevance of psychosocial theories for behaviour change (Hughes, 2004).

Teachers who hold views of this kind are going to have difficulties accepting the validity, or educational utility, of the ADHD concept. The concept of teachers as craft persons evolved from the concept that teaching develops from practice. This means that teaching is not theory led, but rather, the common-sense theories about why a particular pedagogical decision is taken are usually based on experience of what has worked in the past. Teachers refine their teaching repertoires and routines through processes of reflection and, in the initial stages of a teaching career, the teacher will often engage in practices that are an imitation of the behaviours of expert teachers or those they have encountered during their training and initial teaching experience (Morrison and McIntyre, 1968). By the time teachers have reached the stage of being 'expert', they have accumulated a complex repertoire of teaching skills which enables them to manage a bewildering number and range of classroom variables and to make on-the-spot decisions. Brown and McIntyre (1993) illuminated this aspect of teachers' thinking in an intensive study of 16 teachers working in mainstream schools in Scotland. They found that:

The teachers studied all evaluated their teaching in terms of their attainment of normal desirable states of pupil activity, which are steady states of activity seen by teachers as appropriate for pupils at different stages of lessons, and types of progress, including pupils' learning or development, the creation of products and the coverage of work. Both the standards used by teachers in setting their standards for evaluating how well their goals were attained, and the teachers' selection of appropriate actions from their generally extensive repertoires, were strongly influenced by a large number of circumstantial conditions, of which the most salient were those relating to the pupils being taught. (Brown and McIntyre, 1993: 5)

It is the issue of how teachers think about pupils, and how this way of thinking influences the pedagogical decision-making of teachers, that is central to the current chapter.

How teachers think about pupils

When the teachers in Brown and McIntyre's (1993) study talked about pupils, they occasionally focused on characteristics of whole-class groups, but they were most concerned with the particular characteristics of individual pupils or of sub-groups of pupils. According to the teachers in this study, pedagogic decisions were sometimes made on the basis of the teachers' interpretation of the current state of pupil engagement and arousal. They referred to pupils' 'feelings, state of mind, physical well-being or cognition' (ibid. 71), and talked of them being 'switched off', 'tired' or 'giggling', and made adjustments to their manner of lesson delivery on the basis of these perceptions. Brown and McIntyre go on to observe, however, that: 'Although the teachers made frequent mention in this way of how pupils' immediate classroom behaviour imposed Conditions on their teaching, they referred more often to pupils' more enduring characteristics' (Brown and McIntyre, 1993: 72).

These 'more enduring characteristics' included: 'ability (general and specific), attention seeking, self-confidence, lack of interest, motivation, tenacity, attentiveness, gender, maturity, attitudes, disruptive tendencies, laziness, poor grasp of English, noisiness and reticence' (ibid. 73). These characteristics were all seen by the teachers in this study as *stable* characteristics of individual pupils that imposed constraints on the individual teacher's scope for facilitating learning. These findings were replicated and elaborated by Cooper and McIntyre (1996) in a study of teachers in English secondary schools, where after only a few weeks of Year 7, teachers came to apparently stable decisions about the characteristics of their pupils' behaviour, motivation and personal attributes (Cooper and McIntyre, 1996: 133).

The key point to be made here is that mainstream teachers' pedagogical decision-making is strongly influenced by decisions that teachers make about pupils on the basis of fairly limited interaction and observation. These decisions can be understood in terms of Hargreaves et al's (1975) theory of 'typing', by which the teacher places pupils into ready-made categories relating to pupils' perceived ability, behaviour and motivation, and other personal attributes (for example, appearance, gender and so on) (Cooper and McIntyre, 1996). The work of Brown and McIntyre (1993) and Cooper and McIntyre (1996) would further suggest that this 'typing' process is an important element in expert teachers' professional **craft knowledge**, enabling them to make speedy sense of complex circumstances and conditions in busy classroom settings in which there is limited time for extended reflection and analysis.

Effective learning and teaching episodes

Cooper and McIntyre (1996) indicate that both teachers and pupils were in agreement that effective teaching and learning was characterized by:

- teacher-initiated actions that enabled pupils to engage with learning tasks in ways that gave pupils a sense of ownership of learning outcomes

- pupils being given opportunities to incorporate and assimilate new knowledge with existing knowledge

- employing a variety of techniques, including directive approaches, such as storytelling and lecturing, as well as interactive approaches which required students to bring to bear their existing knowledge on tasks, often in group settings

- reactive teaching, where teachers formulate learning foci on the basis of their perceptions and understandings of current pupil state (sometimes abandoning a predetermined lesson plan and pre-set learning objectives, because of their belief that at that particular time the pupils were orientated in a way that was more compatible with an alternative set of activities and learning objectives than those planned).

Both pupils' and teachers' accounts were consistent with social constructivist theories of teaching and learning, such as those proposed by Vygotsky (1987) and Bruner (1987), though research participants did not make explicit reference to these theories, and showed little or no conscious understanding of them.

Teachers' knowledge of effective pedagogy

A major concern to emerge from the application of typing and labelling theories to education, has been the problem of teachers placing limitations on pupils' opportunities for educational engagement based on assumed characteristics about the pupils. Nowhere has this concern been voiced more forcefully than in relation to the phenomenon of Attention Deficit Hyperactivity Disorder (ADHD), which has been dismissed by some commentators as a medical construct that individualizes educational failure and disruptive behaviour (for example Slee, 1995). The effect of such individualization distracts attention from the roles that schools and teachers may play (wittingly or unwittingly) in the exacerbation of learning and behavioural problems.

Whilst 'typing' is an important tool employed by teachers as a practical strategy derived in response to the need to make rough and ready judgements about pupils in order to make necessary pedagogical decisions, teachers may find it helpful:

- if an understanding of ADHD was integrated with the routine way of thinking about the benefit of pupils' learning

■ to make practical use of new theories and insights in their pedagogy by understanding them in terms of routine patterns and pedagogical reasoning

■ to critically explore existing theories to extrapolate existing effective practice that may need refining in the light of new theories.

A study by Monro (1999) sheds further light on ways in which teacher reflection can be stimulated and influenced to produce changes in pedagogical practice. In Monro's study of 32 Australian teachers, the teachers were recruited to a professional development programme that: 'engaged [them in] systematic analysis of their existing knowledge of learning and of their beliefs about learning. They tested these against empirical data collected by them and their colleagues in teaching and against contemporary theories of learning. They mapped their theories into teaching procedures and put these to trial in their classrooms' (Monro, 1999: 154).

Monro gathered observational data on the changes in teacher classroom behaviours, teachers' perceptions of their ability to facilitate effective classroom learning, and qualitative and quantitative data on student performance. The findings of the study were summarized in the following terms:

> the findings support the prediction that involvement in a systematic exploration of the learning process, in which teachers explicate their knowledge of learning, impacts directly on the display of effective teaching procedures and teacher attitudes to learning … [teacher] knowledge becomes more generally useful when it is recorded into an explicit personal theory, tested against a practical data base (the classroom) and mapped into teaching procedures. A key issue in the recoding was the provision of a conceptual framework or scaffold that teachers used to develop their personal explicit theory of learning. (Monro, 1999: 168)

In this case the 'scaffold' was provided by social constructivist theories of learning. Some important points need to be made here about theory and pedagogy:

1. Teaching can be usefully understood as a theory-driven process. However, practical theories are not necessarily articulated explicitly, and are not necessarily falsifiable (and, therefore, testable) in the way that scientific theories are required to be.

2. It is entirely wrong to dismiss the practical theorizing of teachers, simply because it is 'unscientific'. Practical theorizing is at the heart of expert teaching. It is a central component in the professional development of teachers and a major source of insight into the nature of effective teaching. Furthermore, it is a key factor justifying the current renewed interest in teacher autonomy as an important basis for the future development of the teaching profession in complex and fast-moving advanced economies (Johnson and Hallgarten, 2002).

3. Practical theorizing does preclude scientific theorizing. We argue that the processes of teaching become more available to scrutiny and purposive development when practical theorizing is shifted from the tacit to the explicit realm, and opportunities are sensitively created for teachers to incorporate scientific understandings into their reflections on their practical theories.

The rest of this chapter deals with the contribution that various aspects of the theoretical construct of ADHD can make to the development of teachers' pedagogical decision-making processes.

Before we can develop this line of discussion further, however, it is necessary to provide a brief account of ADHD, its nature and antecedents.

How to make your teaching style work for pupils with ADHD

If we accept that ADHD is a bio-psychosocial condition, then we have to acknowledge the mismatch between the cognitive characteristics presented by the child with ADHD and the commonly used behavioural management approach of schools and classrooms throughout the world. The *DSM* diagnostic criteria harbours taken-for-granted assumptions about the kinds of pupil behaviours that are to be expected in properly functioning *classrooms*.

A properly functioning classroom is constrained by the following:

- Pupils from an early age are expected to internalize and behave in accordance with a set of rules that derive from constraints imposed by a teacher-centred, curriculum-focused method of teaching pupils in age-related groups.

- Teacher–pupil ratios create potential problems of social disorder which are met with rules of conduct designed to regulate pupil movement around the classroom and interactions between peers.

- Externally imposed curricula, as opposed to negotiated curricula, assuming a tight relationship between pupil age and cognitive functioning, tend to be managed by teachers in ways that require pupils to follow a lineal programme of tasks at predetermined times and within strict time limits.

It follows from this, that teachers often fulfil the role of 'instructors', providing an estimated 80 per cent of the talk that goes on in classrooms (Sage, 2002). Pupils, therefore, are required to be expert in following complex instructions and internalizing behavioural and cognitive routines which, in turn, are intended to establish patterns of self-regulation which become increasingly important as pupils pass through the higher realms of the curriculum and schooling process. It has long been noted that this factory model of education is by no means the only, or even the most desirable, model of schooling. At its worst it rewards conformity and passivity at the expense of intellectual curiosity, critical debate and creativity (Silberman, 1971). At its best it favours pupils whose cognitive styles favour systematic reflection and abstract lineal thinking. These imposed restrictions impact on classroom functioning and run counter to the cognitive limitations of children whose bio-psychosocial condition imposes limitations on their ADHD. This makes schooling a problematic experience for these pupils and provides a major source of stress to all pupils with attention and activity problems.

Cognitive strategies

The pedagogical task of the teacher is to mediate between these ever-present forces that socially construct problems and exacerbate existing problems for pupils in order to achieve pupil participation to produce desired learning outcomes. The pedagogical thinking of the teacher who is knowledgeable about ADHD will be significantly influenced by the knowledge that an appropriately diagnosed individual will have been judged to demonstrate specific cognitive deficiencies in relation to executive functions. Cognitive deficiencies are contrasted with cognitive distortions (Bracewell, 1995). Bracewell contrasts cognitive distortions and deficits in the following way:

Faulty problem solving processes, skewed perceptual process, information processing errors, and/or irrational beliefs or expectations. In these circumstances the individual is actively processing his or her world but the outcomes of this processing are faulty or at least different from what non-impaired others might conclude from the same information. Cognitive deficiencies can be thought of as cognitive absences. In this case there is no evidence of distortion but rather absence or under-functioning in key cognitive processes. (ibid: 320)

This distinction can be used to inform pedagogical decision-making by directing the teacher towards strategies designed to 'train or reinforce his or her use of the "missing pieces" in his or her cognitive repertoire' (ibid.). Cognitive behavioural therapy (CBT) (Meichenbaum and Goodman, 1971), sometimes referred to as cognitive behaviour modification (CBM), provides the basis for classroom interventions that can be used by teachers. For example:

Child A: Child with cognitive distortion Every time there is a disagreement the child starts fighting with another pupil or throwing something. Therefore to change his or her behaviour you need to change his or her beliefs. This can be done by generating different choices for that situation.

Child B: Child with ADHD The deficits associated with ADHD mean the child has a problem at the processing level, and therefore has limitations with short-term memory. In this case his or her behaviour may appear the same as Child A, but this child's underlying cause of behaviour is different. Therefore, although the desired outcome for each child is the same, that is, change the behaviour, the approach will need to take into account that Child B has a deficit not a distortion.

The teacher therefore may find it useful to consider some of these examples:

■ *Use of internal dialogue*: teaching pupils to use internal dialogue to regulate their thinking and behaviour; this can take the form of rehearsing with pupils desired thinking routines, first through verbalization and then through internal dialogue.

■ *Self-reinforcement of desired behaviours*: self-reinforcement of desired behaviours, self-instruction techniques and problem-solving routines are key parts of this approach. Teachers can facilitate this through direct instruction and modelling (Ervin et al., 1996).

■ *Self-instruction techniques*: self-instruction techniques, which derive from the social constructivist theories of Luria and Vygotsky, are aimed at giving pupils control over their own learning, and can be contrasted with some of the more behaviouristic approaches often associated with ADHD, the aim of which is to extinguish unwanted behaviour and promote behavioural conformity (for example, Goldstein, 1995).

Research evidence for the efficacy of CBT for ADHD is far from conclusive. Reviews by Purdie et al. (2002) and Ervin et al. (1996) report mixed findings. Although it is suggested that school-based programmes tend to be more effective than clinic-based approaches in promoting behavioural change (Ervin et al., 1996), this change is not often generalized to settings outside of the training situation (ibid.).

A review of studies of the effects of self-monitoring strategies on pupils' attention to task by Lloyd and Landrum (1990) concluded that it was generally effective. Lerner and Lowenthal (1994) supported this view and showed that self-instruction and self-monitoring strategies can be effective in reducing key ADHD symptoms of inattention, distractibility, impulsivity, difficulty in following rules and poor social skills. It has been suggested by Ervin et al. (1996) that some of the disappointing research evidence in relation to CBT in connection with ADHD is possibly the result of a failure of some of the interventions to distinguish effectively between cognitive deficits and cognitive distortions (see above). Ervin et al. (1996) indicate that many CBT interventions are based on the erroneous assumption that children with ADHD lack cognitive strategies, rather than the more persuasive view (proposed by Barkley, 1997) that dysfunctions in the operation of their executive functions make it difficult for them to perform the strategies, even when they know them. This suggests that CBT techniques will be more successful if they focus on providing pupils with techniques that enable them to delay and inhibit their responses.

Given that cognitive deficits are believed to be at the heart of ADHD it is clear that the kinds of strategies referred to above are likely to play an important role in pedagogical approaches designed to meet the particular needs of pupils with ADHD. It is also important to note that research reviews which have covered these approaches for pupils with ADHD indicate that the approaches tend to be most effective in promoting appropriate forms of pupil engagement in classrooms, when the approaches are employed by teachers in this setting with a specifically educational focus, as opposed to being carried out by clinicians in off-site settings with a focus on the general regulation of ADHD symptoms (Purdie et al., 2002).

Educational strategies for managing the learning context for pupils with ADHD

In keeping with the specifically cognitive strategies, derived from an understanding of the cognitive deficits associated with ADHD, there is a range of pedagogical approaches used by teachers for supporting pupils with ADHD commonly referred to as 'educational' approaches (DuPaul and Stoner, 1994; Purdie et al., 2002; Zentall, 1995). These approaches are designed to exploit, rather than inhibit, some of the characteristics associated with ADHD. As such, these approaches are consistent with a view of ADHD as a particular cognitive style, rather than a reflection of an underlying deficit. This 'reframing' of ADHD is seen as making an important contribution to the development of positive teacher attitudes towards pupils with ADHD (Cooper and Ideus, 1997; Cooper and O'Regan, 2001a).

Zentall (1995), for example, describes strategies designed to increase the active participation of students with ADHD though the provision of visual motor-tasks:

One such task requires students to write answers to teachers' questions on cards and hold these up for inspection by the teacher. This strategy helps minimize periods of delay between the completion of tasks by pupils and the receipt of teacher feedback.

A study by Zentall and Meyer (1987) found that strategies such as this were associated with improved performance and behaviour of pupils with ADHD when compared with their performance on tasks requiring more passive engagement of students.

Evidence from studies reviewed by DuPaul and Stoner (1994) supports this view, showing that:

> pupils with ADHD respond well to feedback and reinforcement from teachers when the frequency of these interventions is greater than it is for eliciting desired engagement and responses from 'regular' students.

Interventions based on the belief that students with ADHD tend to have an active learning style have been reported as a positive attribution (Hinshaw et al., 1984):

> Their active learning style maximizes opportunities for pupil to engage in role play and kinaesthetic learning tasks which have been shown to increase levels of attention to task in pupils with ADHD and reduce disruptive and impulsive behaviours.

Related to this is the insight that pupils with ADHD are particularly prone to the negative consequences of 'recess deprivation' (Zentall, 1995). Pelligrini and Horvat (1995) found that:

> levels of disruptive behaviour decreased and levels of on task behaviour increased when periods of 'seatwork' were punctuated by frequent periods in which students were required to engage in structured physical activity.

This did not require an increase in the overall amount of recess time provided during a school day, but implies the redistribution of such time throughout the day at regular intervals. Although this study showed improvements for pupils with and without ADHD, Zentall and Smith (1992) found that:

> pupils with ADHD self-reported a greater preference for frequent physical activity than pupils without ADHD.

This provides support for the view that whilst virtually all pupils are likely to benefit from many of the interventions specifically directed at pupils with ADHD, pupils in general are more likely to tolerate the stresses created by certain common but undesirable features of schooling than pupils with ADHD (Cooper and Bilton, 2002).

A major classroom problem associated with ADHD is the tendency of affected pupils to be talkative at inappropriate times. This 'problem' can be exploited for pedagogical purposes by the teacher increasing opportunities for on-task verbal participation by pupils (Zentall, 1995). Studies have found that:

> pupils with ADHD perform better on reading comprehension tasks when they are required to read comprehension passages aloud, rather than silently. (Dubey and O'Leary, 1975)

Also,

> the tendency of pupils with ADHD to dominate verbal interactions with peers in negative ways can be modified by training them to use questioning techniques rather than assertion. (Zentall, 1995)

This technique works best when combined with social skills training (ibid.). Zentall (1995), drawing on empirical evidence provided by Rosenfeld and colleagues, suggests that:

> seating pupils in a semicircle around the teacher, or in small groups produces more on-task verbal participation by pupils with ADHD and more appropriate hand-raising behaviours during whole-class teaching episodes.

Furthermore, there is evidence to support the conclusion that

> reducing the teacher–pupil ratio, in situations involving teacher–group verbal interaction, improves the quality of engagement of pupils with ADHD (ibid.).

This effect is enhanced when teachers provide behavioural models for active listening strategies (Carter and Schostak, 1980).

The twin pedagogical strategies of behavioural modelling and teacher direction are strongly associated with a reduction in pupil inattentiveness and impulsiveness in the classroom and positive academic outcomes. These effects are most powerful when teacher direction involves clear and distinct information about performance, behavioural expectations and expected outcomes.

> Optimal pupil performance is associated with brevity and clarity of sequences of instruction, the accompaniment of verbal instructions with visual cues and the availability of resources that pupils can refer to for reminders of direction and expectations. (DuPaul and Stoner, 1994; Zentall, 1995)

The use of pupils as behavioural and academic models through the careful programming of interaction between the pupil with ADHD and preferred role models is also found to be an effective pedagogical tool. However, it is important that any opportunities for disruption as created by such pupil interaction are controlled by the teacher's use of positive reinforcement for task-appropriate and socially desirable behaviour (Zentall, 1995). In accordance with these findings, Cooper and O'Regan (2001) provide case study material indicating that:

> pupils with ADHD can benefit from taking on the role of peer tutors with younger, less competent pupils. A Key Stage 3 pupil with ADHD showed improved academic self-organizational skills after being required to teach these skills to a Key Stage 2 pupil with learning difficulties.

In a classroom environment in which extraneous stimuli, such as irrelevant noise and other distracters, are limited, and where pedagogical strategies of the type described above are in use, opportunities are created to enable the pupil with ADHD to practise self-pacing.

> Self-pacing, as opposed to external (that is, teacher-directed) pacing is associated with greater accuracy (Zentall, 1995) and pupil self-reported satisfaction (Cooper and Shea, 1998) with learning tasks.

This can usefully extend to providing pupils with ADHD opportunities to remove themselves from classroom situations which they find stressful, to a predetermined quiet area, when the need arises. (DuPaul and Stoner, 1994; Zentall, 1995)

In their the recent meta-analysis of interventions for ADHD, Purdie et al. (2002) found that, in comparison to clinical interventions (such as medication, behaviour and cognitive behavioural therapy, parent training and multi-modal interventions), educational interventions, of the type describe above, were most effective in promoting positive cognitive outcomes.

'Cognitive outcomes' were defined in terms of general cognition (non-specified academic performance), language and reading skills, mathematical skills, IQ and memory functions. Although the overall mean effect size was small (.28), it was concluded that educational interventions were the most effective in producing cognitive improvements. Coupled with the finding that school-based, cognitive interventions were also more effective than clinic-based cognitive interventions, this suggests the central importance of the pedagogical approaches to the amelioration of the negative outcomes of ADHD. Multi-modal approaches (combining medical, psychosocial and educational interventions) were found to be second only to medication in achieving improvements in behaviour, and superior to medication in producing improvements in social functioning.

The focus of this chapter on pedagogy has meant that the issue of medication has not been dealt with. This might be seen as an omission by some readers. Medication is seen by many commentators as the single most important feature of the ADHD phenomenon (Baldwin, 2000; Slee, 1995). The irony of this position is that it assumes a bio-medical definition of ADHD. On the other hand, viewing ADHD from an educational perspective enables us to envision what is possible when schools and teachers adopt ADHD as an educational issue. It has already been suggested in this chapter that ADHD as a debilitating problem is at least in part constructed by the uncritical acceptance of certain assumptions about what the demands of schooling are and should be. It is suggested that the concept of ADHD illuminates these assumptions and thus leads us to important pedagogical insights. It may well be the case that, were these insights to be widely incorporated into the craft knowledge of teachers, the use of medication for pupils with ADHD could be rendered less necessary than is currently assumed, as a means of enabling pupils with ADHD to participate in educational settings.

Having said this, significant obstacles remain. For reasons already outlined, ADHD cannot be dealt with simply through reference to a recipe book. Some of the educational implications of what the evidence base tells us about appropriate pedagogy for pupils with ADHD may well be seen to challenge approaches to teaching and the organization of schools that are well established and underpinned by statutory accountability structures. For example, approaches to pacing and the role of pupil self-direction described above might be seen to be in conflict with Office for Standards in Educations (OFSTED) criteria. Suggestions relating to staff–pupil ratios are bound to strike fear into the heart of fiscally prudent politicians and the managers of LEA budgets. Furthermore, the role of 'typing' in teachers' pedagogical decision-making is problematic. If ADHD is construed as a bio-medical issue then its function may be to encourage teachers to abdicate responsibility for adapting their practice in favour of expecting (or even demanding) medication to be applied in order to adapt the pupil to an unsuitable learning environment. These challenges can only be met through creative ways of educating teachers about ADHD, and enabling them to assimilate knowledge about it into their craft knowledge.

ADHD and nurture groups

Although there are no simple 'off the shelf' solutions to ADHD in the classroom, there is evidence to suggest that nurture groups are a very promising intervention for children with the kinds of behavioural difficulties often associated with ADHD. The classic nurture group is small classes of between 10 and 12 students, located in a mainstream primary or infant school and staffed by two adults, usually a teacher and a teaching assistant (Bennathan and Boxall, 2000). The curriculum is holistic and developmental in design, with classroom activities being carefully designed to match the developmental status of individual children. There is also a very strong emphasis on the development of social, cognitive and emotional self-management skills. Evidence suggests that children who exhibit symptoms of hyperactivity are among those whose behaviour and educational engagement improve significantly during the time that they are in the nurture group (Cooper and Whitehead, 2004). Factors that appear to be relevant to this effect include: the calmness and quietness of the nurture group environment; the setting of individual learning and development targets; the high availability of adult attention; the emphasis on social skills development and the raising of self-esteem. The positive effects of nurture groups on behaviour are most marked after two terms, though improvement in cognitive and social engagement continue into the third term and beyond. Unfortunately, the evidence accrued so far indicates that there are problems in the maintenance of improvements for hyperactive children when the children return to mainstream classes on a full-time basis. This marks these children out from pupils with other disruptive characteristics, who maintain the improvements made in the nurture group when they return to the mainstream.

Pupils with ADHD do well in classroom environments that are managed in ways that acknowledge involuntary difficulties they may have with:

- regulating their attention

- motor activity

- tendency towards impulsiveness.

This could be said of virtually all pupils in most schools throughout the world.

When we look at schooling from the perspective of the individual with ADHD we find fault lines that, when addressed, benefit all pupils. The particular problem here, however, is that the surface difficulties posed by the child with ADHD, which tend to be behavioural, are easily and effectively addressed by medication alone (Purdie et al., 2002). Children with ADHD are often rendered manageable by medication. They are also rendered more amenable to the kinds of pedagogical practices described in this chapter (Barkley, 1990; Cooper and Bilton, 2002). However, it may be the case that in the mainstream classroom the absence of a disruptive behavioural presence may make it unnecessary for the teacher to adapt his or her pedagogical practices in order to promote the optimal educational engagement of the pupil with ADHD. After all, whilst the majority of pupils might benefit from ADHD-friendly pedagogy, they do not necessarily demand it. The majority of pupils, it seems, are able to tolerate classrooms that fall short of the requirements demanded by the unmedicated child with ADHD. If the only realistic choice made available is between medication and exclusion, who can blame the parent (or physician) who opts for medication?

We return, therefore, to a central theme of this chapter: ADHD is to a significant degree constructed by assumptions about what a mainstream classroom and school are meant to look like. How far we are prepared to go in challenging these assumptions will determine what is possible for the child with ADHD and whether or not he or she is best catered for in a mainstream school or a specialist setting. If we are serious about challenging unhelpful assumptions, then we must be prepared to put the necessary resources into educating all teachers about ADHD and providing them with policy-backed opportunities to engage in the pedagogical practices that flow from this.

Key points to remember

◆ Effective teaching and learning strategies for children with ADHD are appropriate and beneficial for all pupils.

◆ ADHD is a deficit with information processing and not a cognitive distortion.

◆ Understanding the limitations imposed by ADHD enables teachers to use new theories and insights to inform decision-making about pedagogy.

◆ A combination of seatwork and physical activity, scaffolding visual motor tasks, teacher feedback and reinforcement is just some of the ways to improve the child's learning.

◆ Self-instruction, self-reinforcement of desired behaviour, and problem-solving routines are just some of the ways to improve the child's behaviour.

HAPTER 8

Food for Thought

- ◆ Changing the course of ADHD
- ◆ Working together to identify contributing factors
- ◆ Working together to support the child to cope with ADHD
  - – Support within school
  - – Support within the home
- ◆ Key points to remember

This book has reviewed the debate over whether ADHD is biological, psychosocial or bio-psychosocial with the findings from a research project which identifies the reality of living with the condition. Throughout the chapters we attempt to justify why ADHD needs to be understood as a bio-psychosocial condition, and why a multidisciplinary approach is needed to support children's educational and social development. Given that between 3 and 5 per cent of school-aged children and young people are affected by ADHD (NICE, 2000), it is imperative that teachers and parents are equipped with the knowledge and skills to work with, and support, these children. Unless support is available, these young people face a lifetime of underachieving, socially and academically, added to which they too, because of the biological predisposition to the condition, face the challenge of parenting a child with ADHD.

Changing the course of ADHD

Children are diagnosed according to which category their behaviour characteristics determine, therefore they will either be described as having, Attention-Deficit/Hyperactivity Disorder, Predominantly Inattentive Type; Attention Deficit Hyperactivity Disorder, Predominantly Hyperactive/Impulsive type; or Attention Deficit Hyperactivity Disorder, Combined Type (see Appendix). In addition, the child may also have coexisting behavioural difficulties such as Oppositional Defiant Disorder (ODD) or Conduct Disorder (CD). However, despite these categories, the message to parents and teachers is that the child has a diagnosis of ADHD. Therefore, in theory, you could have a class of children all with a diagnosis of ADHD, but with different behavioural characteristics. The purpose for posing such a scenario is to emphasize the individuality of ADHD. If we accept the importance of perceiving the child with ADHD as an individual rather than a bundle of ADHD characteristics, then we can begin to recognize where to target the support. How this will be achieved is the area that needs to be determined by the support team.

It could be argued that we are all a product of bio-psychosocial influences, so what makes children with ADHD so different from any other children? What makes the difference is society's perception of what is acceptable and non-acceptable behaviour. In today's society, we define the symptoms of ADHD as a recognized psychiatric condition (APA, 1994), a condition that affects academic and social development. On the other hand, this bio-psychosocial condition, pervasive across two or more situations, and likely to progress into adulthood and beyond (Hinshaw 1994), is perceived as warranting a mainstream education. The previous chapters emphasize that government proposals encourage inclusive education and are committed to interagency working. They advocate that partnerships across health and education should include involving the client in the decision-making, to ensure they receive appropriate individual care and support to meet their individual needs.

Why is it, then, that despite such proposals we find that:

1. Interagency working is not evident for children with ADHD?

2. Children with ADHD do not have a voice in the assessment or decision-making process?

If we accept that ADHD is the result of interplay between biological-psychological and social factors, our perceptions will alter to embrace ADHD in its wider context. We can begin to accept, too, that the child is not simply a child that needs medication, neither are they a child whose parents have failed to apply discipline. Teachers, clinicians and parents can begin to address the above by asking themselves these questions:

1. How can *we* ensure that *we* work together, with the child to identify the bio-psychosocial factors contributing to ADHD?

2. How can *we* best work together to support the child to cope with ADHD?

Working together to identify contributing factors

Pharmacological medication can redress an imbalance in brain chemistry and suppress, temporarily, hyperactive and impulsive behaviour, and behavioural interventions can be applied in school and in the home. But the limitations of medication and behavioural management approaches used in isolation (mentioned in previous chapters) identify the need for parents and professionals to share their understanding about ADHD and to co-ordinate their support in order to provide a consistent message to the child.

The client-centred approach is at the heart of government proposals. This approach, for children with ADHD, places the child at the centre of service provision. Making this a reality requires interagency working and children to become part of the assessment and decision-making process.

One reason that professionals are reluctant to share knowledge with other professionals is that teachers, special needs teachers, educational psychologists, clinical psychologists and clinicians are specialists within their own fields and have undergone educational and training programmes that prioritize a micro perspective. Therefore, they consider the behaviour of ADHD to lie within the context of their specialism. As a consequence, sharing information and resources across professional boundaries is a new phenomenon for professional groups. Working collaboratively is a government initiative that needs to be endorsed at the local level and adopted within schools, hospitals and clinics. Support for interagency working must also come from regulatory bodies and the Quality Assurance Agency (QAA) of institutions. If services are to provide the type of co-ordinated support required for ADHD, then further training in the form of continual professional development is required to provide professions with the knowledge, skills and attitudes necessary to work across professional and organizational boundaries. There has to be recognition, too, that working across professional boundaries, may involve adjustment being made to existing services and the delivery of these services.

One way that schools can begin to move in the direction of interagency working is to begin working with parents, making sure that the line of communication within schools is clear and that correspondence with parents encourages them to express concerns and ideas. It might be useful for schools to have a policy that provides parents with clear information about 'what to do if they have a concern about their child's behaviour', enabling them to be clear about the type of information school needs, who they give the information to and what they can expect from taking these steps.

It might be helpful if:

- the policy provides clear directions for parents about how and who to contact in the initial stages

- parents are given a strategy that outlines the process in which issues are dealt with, including the people dealing with specific issues

- parents are provided with a child assessment questionnaire (based on the model in Chapter 6) following their initial contact, along with details of who to return this to and the next stage of the process

- the teacher meets with the parent after he or she makes initial contact with school

- the teacher provides the parent with information about the way the child functions in school (based on the model in Chapter 6)

- the teacher and parent agree to meet on a regular basis, and to involve others as is found appropriate to the child's needs (depending on the outcome of the models used).

Typically, parents of children with ADHD will have tried for years, often alone, to manage their child's behaviour. They may have tried diets, become members of local ADHD support groups, read available literature about the symptoms and tried various strategies to minimize symptoms. Many may not have tried anything, thinking instead that the behaviour is the result of external environmental factors such as school management or relationships with peers, or that it is a biological condition that the child will outgrow. It may have occurred to some parents that their child is displaying a behavioural pattern similar to that of themselves or their partner, and for this reason they may feel inadequate in providing support. Teachers can gain important insight by talking to parents, not only about the type of support the child receives in the home but also the interplay between the home and school environment. In return they can offer parents and the child much in the way of co-operation and support. Involving the child in this partnership is important on two fronts; first it alerts the child to the support structure available and, secondly, it provides the child with a clear channel through which to voice their experiences and to inform their support team on the progress or limitations of interventions.

This type of partnership-working can in turn inform policy. Evaluation of service provision in meeting the needs of the client can inform and influence the decision-making within health authorities and education authorities over how education and training programmes for professions can enhance interagency working and the provision of children's services.

Working together to support the child to cope with ADHD

Children with ADHD are individuals who need an individual framework of support, such as that offered by the bio-psychosocial model, to guide those responsible for their social and educational development. Galloway warns that 'a report on a child's difficulties is inevitably one-sided if it does not also comment on the social and educational context' (Galloway, 2001: 153). In other words, a collaborative approach in itself is inefficient if it does not address the wider concepts related to the child's environment. Without clear guidelines, schools can only offer children with ADHD the provision and skills available for all children, and, although a collaborative approach is suggested, its organization and implementation are implied not explicit. Adding to the school's difficulties is the present category of ADHD, which determines medical provision. Whilst this is a useful concept for the medical profession, it is less useful for educational services to direct provision.

The proposed models in Chapter 6 provide the framework for exploring the support required, and the process by which this occurs. However, there are a number of additional areas that can provide support for staff, parents and children, both in the home and classroom:

> **Area 1** Increase your understanding about ADHD as an important first step.
> Research the diagnosis of ADHD, the cause and the treatments that are evolving, and you need to be aware of changes within these areas to understand how best to support the child and his or her family. In applying the problem-based model in Chapter 6, your understanding will be explored and extended through the interaction with others, and through your search for additional information about the condition. Without up-to-date information it is not possible to disentangle the facts from the myths and it is therefore impossible to provide a co-ordinated and consistent service of support across agencies.

Area 2 Consider how you could enhance your communication links with other colleagues about ADHD. What could you learn from the child's parents? What could you learn from other teaching colleagues? What could you learn from the clinician who made the diagnosis? What could you learn from the child? How does your understanding compare with the information the child gives to you and his or her parents? What could the clinician, colleagues and the child's parents learn from you? How can you establish a link to these people, a link that can be developed and maintained over the period it will be required? This includes following the child's progress through different classes and schools.

Area 3 You need to consider in what way the child's academic, social, emotional and moral development is impaired. What internal and external factors contribute to this impairment? What have you noticed that exacerbates or inhibits the child's behavioural difficulties? How can local policy and strategy plans support the needs you are identifying? How are you going to evaluate the effectiveness of your support system? How are you going to inform others about the effectiveness and limitations of your support system?

Area 4 The purpose behind providing support for the child with ADHD is not just to improve in all areas of his or her development. The child with ADHD needs ultimately to be able to function without support; in other words, to be capable of accepting and working with their strengths and limitations, having developed the knowledge and skills necessary to function well, and independently, in society.

Support within school

Whilst it is recognized that teachers are busy delivering a national curriculum, consider the following and reflect on how you could change the classroom or your teaching approach to accommodate these.

- Keep the child calm.

- Avoid confrontational situations.

- Show the child respect.

- Avoid situations where the child is picked on/bullied.

- Listen to the child and his or her concerns.

- Consider when the child is working at his or her best.

- Consider the child's maximum length of concentration.

- Keep noise levels to a minimum/avoid distraction.

- Keep instructions to a minimum/one at a time.

- Provide reassurance on tasks.

- Split tasks up/allow child to return to the task (break it down).

- Enable them to complete task (as above).

- Offer alternative mental stimulation when the child is distracted.

- Scaffold the child's work.

- Provide clear guidance, verbal and written.

- Be consistent with verbal and written instruction.

- Be consistent with discipline and with goals.

- Provide routine.

- Provide outlets for active behaviour.

- Keep any change to a minimum.

- Prepare the child for any change/teacher/lesson and so on.

- Avoid making the child's limitations apparent to other children.

- Be sensitive to the child's limitations.

- Provide a clear structure in the class and school.

- Provide clear boundaries in class and school.

Support within the home

Whilst it is recognized that parents are juggling jobs, a home and probably other children, it is counterproductive for a child to receive support within school if this cannot be continued in the home. For many parents their child's behaviour will have formed a pattern; the norm for the child and the norm for the parent. Changing this behaviour will demand effort on behalf of the parent and on behalf of the teacher, who needs to inform and support the parent through this transitional period. For example, teachers can encourage parents to:

- set aside time to work with the child/encourage them to do their homework

- prepare a quiet time/area that is conducive to the way the child learns in class

- avoid confrontational situations

- allow the child a calming down period in times of distress

- distract the child from dysfunctional behaviour

- promote their positive characteristics

- provide structure during holidays so that they know what is expected of them

- provide boundaries that they understand

- encourage organizational and timekeeping skills by setting small tasks

- find ways of promoting their self-esteem

- encourage outlets for active behaviour.

The aim for teachers and parents is not only to provide support for the child so that his or her academic and social development improves; it is to encourage the child to develop coping strategies for later life. When faced with situations that challenge their emotional and behavioural difficulties, these children need to be competent in ways of minimizing their difficulties. Whether this means maintaining regular medication, removing themselves from a confrontational situation or letting off steam in the gym, children with ADHD have to learn the rules of society and how to live within these.

An added benefit of ensuring that the child with ADHD has the knowledge and skills to live a normal and independent life is that, when they themselves become parents, they can transfer these to their own children.

Receiving a diagnosis of ADHD is a blow to any child and to any parent, but making this situation worse is finding out that a diagnosis in itself cannot change the child's behaviour. For change to happen there has to be appropriate and sustained intervention and support. This requires a change to the way teachers and other professions perceive ADHD and a change in the way they work to provide co-ordinated and consistent services. It is the responsibility of the stakeholders to enable staff to work collaboratively across professional boundaries and to provide the necessary training and resources for this to happen. The governing body and the Quality Assurance Agency need to endorse guidelines for schools to adopt a culture of interagency working. Schools need to prepare a strategy, based on these guidelines, that informs all teaching staff about how they are to work across professional boundaries and how they are to implement the necessary changes to their work environment and work ethic. Teachers need to feel competent in knowing that they have the backing of their colleagues, and it is schools, and ultimately the teachers, who are responsible for ensuring that all children with ADHD receive the education they deserve.

Key points to remember

◆ Changing the child's behaviour will take time.

◆ Medication alone will not provide the child with sufficient support to change his or her behaviour.

◆ Partnership working to complement the effects of medication and to shape the child's environment is needed.

◆ It is not enough to understand what ADHD is. You need to understand the child as an individual.

◆ Involving the child is essential for you to support his or her limitations and strengths and to enable him or her to work with you.

◆ Partnership working across the home and school setting is important if the child is to receive consistent and co-ordinated support.

APPENDIX: DIAGNOSTIC CRITERIA FOR ATTENTION DEFICIT HYPERACTIVE DISORDER

A (1) Inattention: At least six of the following symptoms of inattention have persisted for at least six months to a degree that is maladaptive and inconsistent with developmental level:

(a) often fails to give close attention to details or makes careless mistakes in schoolwork, work, or other activities

(b) often has difficulty sustaining attention in tasks or play activities

(c) often does not seem to listen to what is being said to him or her

(d) often does not follow through on instructions and fails to finish schoolwork, chores or duties in the workplace (not due to oppositional behaviour or failure to understand instructions)

(e) often has difficulty organizing tasks and activities

(f) often avoids or expresses reluctance about, or has difficulties in, engaging in tasks that require sustained mental effort (such as schoolwork or homework)

(g) often loses things necessary for tasks or activities (for example, school assignments, pencils, books, tools, or toys)

(h) is often easily distracted by extraneous stimuli

(i) is often forgetful in daily activities.

A (2) Hyperactivity-impulsivity: At least six of the following symptoms of hyperactivity-impulsivity have persisted for at least six months to a degree that is maladaptive and inconsistent with developmental level:

Hyperactivity

(a) often fidgets with hands or feet or squirms in seat

(b) leaves seat in classroom or in other situations in which remaining seated is expected

(c) often runs about or climbs excessively in situations where it is inappropriate (in adolescents or adults, may be limited to subjective feelings of restlessness)

(d) often has difficulty playing or engaging in leisure activities quietly

(e) is always 'on the go' and acts as if 'driven by a motor'

(f) often talks excessively.

Impulsivity

(g) often blurts out answers to questions before the questions have been completed

(h) often has difficulty waiting in line or awaiting turn in games or group situations

(i) often interrupts or intrudes on others (for example, butts into others' conversations or games).

B.   Some symptoms that cause impairment were present before age 7.

C.   Some symptoms that cause impairment must be present in two or more settings (for example, at school, work and at home).

D.   There must be clear evidence of clinically significant impairment in social, academic or occupational functioning.

E.   Does not occur exclusively during the course of a Pervasive Development Disorder, Schizophrenia or other Psychiatric Disorder and is not better accounted for by a Mood Disorder, Anxiety Disorder, Dissociative Disorder or a Personality Disorder.

Attention Deficit Hyperactivity Disorder, predominantly Inattentive type: If criterion A(1) is met but not criterion A(2) for the past six months.

Attention Deficit Hyperactivity Disorder, predominantly Hyperactive/Impulsive type: If criterion A(2) is met but not criterion A(1) for the past six months.

Attention Deficit Hyperactivity Disorder, Combined type: If both criterion – A(1) and A(2) – are met for the past six months.

Source: American Psychiatric Association (1994).

GLOSSARY

Here are some of the terms you will meet in this book.

ADHD The characteristics of Attention Deficit Hyperactive Disorder are set out by the American Psychiatric Association and form the diagnosis of ADHD.

Behaviour Actions that can be observed rather than implied from our interpretation of events.

Bio-psychosocial Perceiving behaviour to be influenced by biological, psychological and social factors.

Cognitive Our reasoning abilities, memory, knowledge and understanding.

Cognitive behavioural therapy CBT aims to help change how you think (cognitive) and what you do (behaviour). It focuses on current problems by seeking ways to improve your state of mind.

Co-morbidity A synergy of conditions whereby one disorder is likely to coexist with another disorder.

Craft knowledge A teacher's personal knowledge and skills gained from their experience of teaching and enabling them to make competent judgements in complex situations.

Dopamine Dopamine is a type of neurotransmitter, a chemical messenger that affects the brain processes that control movement and emotional response. It is thought that this neurotransmitter might be responsible for the symptoms of ADHD.

Educational engagement Refers to the synergy between the learning process and the learning experience in enabling the child to achieve.

Empowerment A means of helping a person acquire the relevant understanding and skills to take control of a situation or decision-making for themselves.

Executive functions Executive functions describe a unique set of mental functions by the prefrontal lobes of the cerebral cortex. They impact on cognitive and emotional functioning and, more specifically, cognitive inhibition and initiation, self-regulation and motor output.

Hedonist behaviour Observed in people who act in a calculated and self-regulated way to derive pleasure.

Heterogeneity It is thought that the causal factors for the symptoms of ADHD are the result of an interplay between numerous biological, psychological and social factors.

Hyperactivity Extreme activity as opposed to normal active behaviour in that a child is constantly 'on the go', moving around, touching or playing with whatever is in sight, or talking incessantly.

Hyperkinetic The term hyperkinetic is used by some clinicians to describe ADHD.

Impulsiveness Impulsiveness refers to a child who acts without thinking about the consequences. They may blurt out answers, even when inappropriate, make quick decisions without considering the consequences and find themselves spending money they do not have.

Inattention Inattention refers to the child's inability to sustain or inability to select to pay attention.

Inclusive education An opportunity for all children, with or without disabilities, to receive and be included in mainstream education.

Multidisciplinary Involving a number of disciplines in the assessment, diagnosis and support of a child with ADHD.

National Institute for Clinical Excellence NICE provides guidelines to the National Health Service in England and Wales on the use of methylphenidate for this condition.

Neurological Behaviour that is the result of the mechanisms of the nerve pathways and impulses that make up the neural network in the body.

Pedagogical The principles and process of teaching to include the activities of educating pupils and the impact this has on their knowledge and skills.

Perspectives An individual's understanding of a situation, or behaviour.

Psycho-stimulants Psycho-stimulant medication is thought to be beneficial in improving attention span, impulse control and in reducing motor activity.

Self-regulation The ability to control one's behaviour.

REFERENCES

American Psychiatric Association (APA) (1968) *Diagnostic and Statistical Manual of Mental Disorders.* 2nd edn. Washington, DC: APA.

American Psychiatric Association (APA) (1980) *Diagnostic and Statistical Manual of Mental Disorders.* 3rd edn. Washington, DC: APA.

American Psychiatric Association (APA) (1987) *Diagnostic and Statistical Manual of Mental Disorders.* 3rd revd edn. Washington, DC: APA.

American Psychiatric Association (APA) (1994) *Diagnostic and Statistical Manual of Mental Disorders.* 4th edn. Washington, DC: APA.

Anastopoulos, A. (1999) 'AD/HD', in S. Netherton, C. Holmes and C. Walker (eds), *Child and Adolescent Psychological Disorders: A Comprehensive Textbook.* Oxford: Oxford University Press.

Anderson, E.S., Lennox, A. and Paterson, S. (2003) 'Learning from lives: a model for health and social care education in the wider community context', *Medical Education*, 37: 1–10.

Angold, A., Costello, E. and Erkanli, A. (1999) 'Comorbidity', *Journal of Child Psychology and Psychiatry*, 40 (1): 57–88.

Appleton, P.L., Boll, V., Everett, J.M,. Kelly, A.M., Meredith, K.H. and Paynes, T.G. (1997) 'Beyond child development centres: care coordination for children with disabilities', *Child: Care, Health and Development*, 23 (1): 29–40.

Armstrong, D., Galloway, D. and Tomlinson, S. (1993) 'Assessing special educational needs: the child's contribution', *British Educational Research Journal*, 9(2): 121–31.

Baldwin, S. (2000) 'Head to head' (with Paul Cooper), *Journal of Emotional and Behavioural Difficulties*, 13(12): 623–5.

Barkley, R. (1990) *AD/HD: A Handbook for Diagnosis and Treatment*, ed. Dr. R. Barkley. New York: Guilford Press.

Barkley, R.A (1997) 'Understanding AD/HD and self-control: social and clinical implications', in *AD/HD and the Nature of Self Control.* New York: Guilford.

Barkley, R.A. (1998) *Attention deficit hyperactivity disorder: A handbook for diagnosis and treatment.* 2nd edn. New York: Guilford Press.

Barkley, R.A., DuPaul, G.J. and McMurray, M.B. (1990) 'A comprehensive evaluation of attention deficit disorder with and without hyperactivity', *Journal of Consulting and Clinical Psychology*, 58: 775–89.

Bax, M.C.O. and Whitmore, K. (1991) 'District handicap teams in England, 1983–8', *Archives of Diseases in Childhood*, 66(5): 656–64.

Bennathan, M. and Boxall, M. (2000) *Effective Intervention in Primary Schools: Nurture Groups.* London: Fulton.

Bennathan, M. and Boxall, M. (2003) *Effective Intervention in Primary Schools: Nurture Group.* London: Fulton.

Bohline, D.S. (1985) 'Intellectual and affective characteristics of attention deficit disordered children', *Journal of Learning Disabilities*, 18: 604–8.

Booth, T. and Ainscow, M. (1998) *From Them to Us.* London: Routledge.

Booth, T., Ainsow, M., Black-Hawkins, K., Vaughn, M. and Shaw, I. (2000) *Index for Inclusion: Developing Learning and Participation in Schools.* Bristol: CSIE.

Bracewell, L. (1995) 'Cognitive-behavioural approaches in the classroom', in S. Goldstein (ed.), *Understanding and Managing Children's Classroom Behaviour*, New York: John Wiley and Sons.

British Psychological Society (BPS) (1996) *AD/HD: A Psychological Response to an Evolving Concept*. Leicester: BPS.

British Psychological Society (BPS) (2000) *AD/HD: Guidelines and Principles for Successful Multi-Agency Working*. Leicester: BPS.

Brown, S. and McIntyre, D. (1993) *Making Sense of Teaching*. Buckingham: Open University Press.

Bruner, J. (1987) 'The transactional self', in J. Bruner and H. Haste (eds), *Making Sense*. London: Methuen.

Buhrmester, D., Whalen, C.K., Henker, B., MacDonald, V. and Hinshaw, S.P. (1992) 'Pro-social behaviour in hyperactive boys: effects of stimulant medication and comparison with normal boys', *Journal of Abnormal Child Psychology*, 20: 103–19.

Burrows, H.S. and Tamblyn, R.M. (1980) *Problem-based Learning: An Approach to Medical Education*. New York: Springer Publishing.

Campbell, S.B. and Ewing, L.J. (1990) 'Follow up of hard to manage preschoolers', *Journal of Child Psychology and Psychiatry*, 31: 879–89.

Cantwell, D. (1975) *The Hyperactive Child: Diagnosis management and current research*. New York: Spectrum.

Carter, E.N and Schostak, D.A. (1980) 'Imitation in the treatment of the hyperkinetic behaviour syndrome', *Journal of Clinical Child Psychology*, 9: 63–6.

Cooper, P. (1993) 'Field relations and the problem of authenticity in researching participants perceptions of teaching and learning in classrooms', *British Educational Research Journal*, 19(4): 323–38.

Cooper, P. (2001) *We Can Work It Out: What Works in Alternative Provision for Children with Social, Emotional and Behavioural Difficulties*. London: Barnardo's.

Cooper, P. (2006) *Promoting Positive Pupil Engagement: Educating Pupils with Social, Emotional and Behavioural Difficulties*. Malta: Agenda.

Cooper, P. and Bilton, K.M. (2002) *Attention Deficit/Hyperactivity Disorder: A Practical Guide for Teachers*. 2nd edn. London: David Fulton.

Cooper, P. and Ideus, K. (1997) *Attention Deficit/Hyperactivity Disorder: Medical, Educational and Cultural Issues*. 2nd revd edn. East Sutton: Association of Workers for Children with Emotional and Behavioural Difficulties.

Cooper, P. and McIntyre, D. (1996) *Effective Teaching and Learning: Teachers' and Students' Perspectives*. Milton Keynes: Open University Press.

Cooper, P. and Shea, T. (1997) 'ADHD from the inside: an empirical study of young people's perceptions of the experience of ADHD' in P. Cooper and K. Bilton (eds), *Pupils with AD/HD: Research, Experience, Practice and Opinion*. London: David Fulton.

Cooper, P. and Whitehead, D. (2004) *The Effectiveness of Nurture Groups: Evidence from a National Research Study*. Leicester: University of Leicester.

Cooper, P.W and O'Regan, F. (2001) 'Ruby Tuesday: case study of student with AD/HD', *Emotional and Behavioural Difficulties*, 6(4): 265–9.

Cooper, P.W. and O'Regan, F. (2001a) *Educating Students with AD/HD: A Teachers' Handbook*. London: Routledge.

Cooper, P.W. and Shea, T. (1998) 'Pupils perception of AD/HD', *Emotional and Behavioural Difficulties*, 3(3): 36–48.

Cooper. P.W., Drummond, M., Hart, S., Lovey, J. and McLaughlin, C. (2000) *Positive Alternatives to Exclusion*. London: Routledge.

Department for Education and Employment (DfEE) (1989) *Children Act*. London: DfEE.

Department for Education and Employment (DfEE) (1993) *Education Act*. London: HMSO.

Department for Education and Employment (DfEE) (1997) *Excellence for All Children*. London: HMSO.

Department for Education and Skills (DfES) (2001) *Code of Practice on Special Educational Needs*. London: HMSO.

Department for Education and Skills (DfES) (2001a) *Inclusive Schools: Children with Special Educational Need*. London: HMSO.

Department for Education and Skills (DfES) (2003) *Every Child Matters*. Green Paper. London: Stationery Office.

Department for Education and Skills (DfES) (2004) *Every Child Matters, Change for Children*. London: Stationery Office.

Department of Education and Science (DES) (1978) *Special Educational Needs* (Warnock Report). Cmnd. 7212. London: HMSO.

Department of Health (DoH) (1998) *Our Healthier Nation*. London: HMSO.

Douglas, V.I. (1983) 'Attention and cognitive problems', in M. Rutter (ed.), 'Dosage effects and individual responsivity to methylphenidate in attention deficit disorder', *Journal of Child Psychology and Psychiatry*, 29: 453–75.

Dubey, D.R. and O'Leary, S.G. (1975) 'Increasing reading comprehension of two hyperactive children: preliminary investigation', *Perceptual and Motor Skills*, 41: 691–4.

DuPaul, G. and Stoner, G. (1994) *AD/HD in the Schools*. New York: Guilford.

Dyson, A., Howes, A. and Roberts, B. (2002) *A Systematic Review of the Effectiveness of School-Level Actions for Promoting Participation by All Students (EPPI-Centre Review)*. London: EPPI.

Ervin, R.A., Bankert, C.L. and Dupaul, G.J. (1996) 'Treatment of attention-deficit hyperactivity disorder', in M.A. Reinecke and F.M. Datillo (eds), *Cognitive Therapy with Children and Adolescents*. New York: Guilford Press. pp. 38–61.

Farrington, D. (1990) 'Implications of criminal career research for the prevention of offending', *Journal of Adolescence*, 13: 93–113.

Field, R., and West, M. (1995) 'Teamwork in primary health care: 2 perspectives from practice', *Journal of Interprofessional Care*, 9(2): 123–9.

Fischer, M., Barkley, R.A., Edelbrock, C.S. and Smallish, L. (1990) 'The adolescent outcome of hyperactive children diagnosed by research criteria: II. Academic, attentional and neuropsychological status', *Journal of Consulting and Clinical Psychology*, 58: 580–88.

Frith, U. (1992) 'Cognitive development and cognitive deficit', *The Psychologist*, 5: 13–19.

Galloway, D. (2001) 'Educational reform and the mental health of vulnerable children and young people', *Child Psychology and Psychiatry Review*, 6(4): 150–6.

Goldstein, S. (1995) 'Understanding and assessing AD/HD and related educational disorders', in P. Cooper and K. Ideus (eds), *AD/HD: Educational, Medical and Cultural Issues*. East Sutton: Association of Workers for Children with Emotional and Behavioural Difficulties.

Greenhill, L.L. (1995) 'Attention deficit hyperactivity disorder: the stimulants', *Child and Adolescent Psychiatric Clinics*, 4(1), 123–68.

Greenhill, L.L., and Ford, R.E. (2002) 'Childhood attention deficit hyperactivity disorder: pharmacological treatments', in P.E. Nathan and J.M. Gorman (eds), *A Guide to Treatments that Work*. 2nd edn. Oxford: Oxford University Press. pp. 25–55.

Guzzo, R.A., and Shea, G.P (1992) 'Group performance and intergroup relations in organisations', in M.A. West and J. Slater (eds) (1997) *Teamworking in Primary Health Care: A Review of its Effectiveness*. Research report prepared for the Health Education Authority.

Hall, D. (1997) 'Child development teams: are they fulfilling their purpose?', *Child: Care, Health, and Development*, 23(1): 87–99.

Hargreaves, D.H., Hester, S.K. and Mellor, F.J. (1975) *Deviance in Classrooms*. London: Routledge and Kegan Paul.

Hayden, C. (1997) 'Exclusion from primary school: children in need and children with special educational need', *Emotional and Behavioural Difficulties*, 2(3): 36–44.

Hinshaw, S. (1994). *Attention Deficits and Hyperactivity in Children*. London, New York and New Delhi: Sage.

Hinshaw, S.P., Henker, B. and Whalen, C.K. (1984) 'Cognitive-behavioural and pharmacologic interventions for hyperactive boys: comparative and combined effects', *Journal of Consulting and Clinical Psychology*, 52: 739–49.

Hughes, L. (2004) 'Perspectives on living with children with attention deficit hyperactive disorder: the rhetoric and the reality', PhD thesis, University of Bradford, Bradford, UK.

Hughes, L.A. and Lucas, J. (1997) 'An evaluation of problem-based learning in the multi-professional education curriculum for the health professions', *Journal of Interprofessional Care*, 11(1): 77–88.

Johnson, M. and Hallgarten, J. (2002) *From Victims of Change to Agents of Change: The Future of the Teaching Profession*. London: Policy Studies Institute.

Kelly, G.A. (1955) *The Psychology of Personal Constructs*. New York: Norton.

Klein, R.G. and Mannuzza, S. (1991) 'Long-term outcome of hyperactive children: a review', *Journal of the American Academy of Child and Adolescent Psychiatry*, 30: 383–7.

Lerner, J. and Lowenthal, B. (1994) 'Attention deficit disorders', *Learning Disabilities*, 4: 1–8.

Lloyd, J.W. and Landrum, T.J. (1990) 'Self-recording of attending to task: treatment components and generalization of effects', in T.E. Scruggs and B.Y.L. Wong (eds), *Intervention Research in Learning Disabilities*. New York: Springer-Verlag. pp. 235–62.

Mariani, M.A., and Barkley, R.A. (1997) 'Neoropsychological and academic functioning in pre school boys with attention deficit hyperactivity disorder', *Developmental Neuropsychology*, 13(1): 111–29.

McManus, M. (1989) *Troublesome Behaviour in the Classroom*. London: Routledge.

McMullen, G., Painter, D. and Casey, T. (1994) 'Assessment and treatment of AD/HD in children', in L. VendeCreek, S. Knapp and T. Jackson (eds), *Innovations in Clinical Practice*. Sarasotat, FL: Professional Resource Press.

Meichenbaum, D. and Goodman, J. (1971) 'Training impulsive children to talk to themselves: a means of developing self control', *Journal of Abnormal Psychology*, 77: 115–26.

Miller, C., Ross, N. and Freeman, M. (1999) *Shared Learning and Clinical Teamwork: New Directions in Education for Multiprofessional Practice*. London: English National Board for Nursing, Midwifery and Health Visiting.

Monro, J. (1999) 'Learning more about learning improves teacher effectiveness', *Journal of Emotional and Behavioural Difficulties* 10(2): 151–71.

Morrison, A. and McIntyre, D. (1968) *Teachers and Teaching*. Harmondsworth: Penguin.

MTA Cooperative Group (1999) 'A 14 month randomised clinical trial of treatment strategies for attention-deficit/hyperactivity disorder', *Archives of General Psychiatry*, 56:1073–86.

National Institute of Clinical Excellence (NICE) (2000) *Guidance on the Use of Methyphenidate for AD/HD*. London: NICE.

National Institute of Clinical Excellence (NICE) (2002) *Guidelines on Methylphenidate for AD/HD*, available at www.nice.org.uk.

Nigg, J., and Hinshaw, S. (1998), 'Parent personality traits and psycho pathology associated with antisocial behaviors in childhood AD/HD', *Journal of Child Psychology and Psychiatry*, 39(2): 145–59.

Norwich, B. (1993) *Special Needs in Ordinary Schools: Reappraising Special Needs Education*. 2nd edn. London: Cassell.

Øvretveit, J. (1993) *Coordinating Community Care: Multidisciplinary Teams and Care Management*. Milton Keynes: Open University Press.

Palmer, E. and Finger, S. (2001) 'An early description of ADHD: Dr Alexander Crichton and "mental restlessness"', *Child Psychology and Psychiatry Review*, 6(2): 66–73.

Pelham, W.E. (1999) 'The NIMH multimodal treatment study for attention deficit hyperactivity disorder: just say yes to drugs alone?', *Canadian Journal of Psychiatry*, 44(December): 981–90.

Pellegrini, A. and Horvat, M. (1995) 'A developmental contextualist critique of AD/HD', *Educational Researcher*, 24(1): 13–20.

Place, M., Wilson, J., Martin, E. and Hulsmeier, J. (2000) 'The frequency of emotional and behaviour disturbance in an EBD school', *Child Psychology and Psychiatry Review*, 5(2): 76–80.

Plomin, R., Owen, M.J., and McGuffin, P. (1994) 'The genetic basis of complex human behaviours', *Science*, 264: 1733–9.

Purdie, N., Hattie, J. and Carroll, A. (2002) 'A review of the research on interventions for AD/HD: what works best?', *Review of Educational Research*, 72(1): 61–99.

Rose, S. (2004) 'The new brain sciences', in D. Rees and S. Rose (eds), *The New Brain Sciences: Perils and Promises*. Cambridge: Cambridge University Press.

Roy, D.F. (1991) 'Improving recall by eyewitnesses through the cognitive interview', *The Psychologist*, September (4): 398–400.

Rutter, M. (2001) 'Child psychiatry in the era following sequencing of the genome', in F. Levy and D.A. Hay (eds), *Attention, Genes and AD/HD*. Hove: Brunner-Routledge. pp. 225–48.

Sage, R. (2002) 'Start talking and stop misbehaving: teaching pupils to communicate, think and act appropriately', *Emotional and Behavioural Difficulties*, 7(2), 85–96.

Schachar, R., Tannock, R., Cunningham, C. and Corkum, P. (1997) 'Behavioral, situational, and temporal effects of treatment of AD/HD with methylphenidate', *Journal of the American Academy of Child & Adolescent Psychiatry*, 36(6): 754–63.

Schostack, J. (1982) *Maladjusted Schooling*. Lewes: Falmer.

Sebba, J. and Sachdev, D. (1997) *What Works in Inclusive Education?* London: Barnardo's.

Sergeant, J. (1995) 'Hyperkinetic disorder revisited', in J. Sergeant (ed.), *Eunythydis: European Approaches to Hyperkinetic Disorder*. Amsterdam: Sergeant.

Sergeant, J.A. and Scholten, C.A. (1985) 'On resource strategy limitation in hyperactivity: cognitive impulsivity reconsidered', *Journal of Child Psychology and Psychiatry*, 26: 97–109.

Silberman, C. (1971) *Crisis in the Classroom*. New York: Random House.

Slee, R. (1995) *Changing Theories and Practices of Discipline*. London: Falmer.

Smith, C. and Laslett, R. (1993) *Effective Classroom Management*. London: Routledge.

Sonuga-Barke, E., Lamparelli, M., Stevenson, J., Thompson, M. and Henry, A. (1994) 'Behaviour problems and preschool intellectual attainment: the association of hyperactivity and conduct problems', *Journal of Child Psychology and Psychiatry*, 35(July): 949–60.

Sonuga-Barke, E., Taylor, E. and Hepenstall, E. (1992) 'Hyperactivity and delay aversion II: the effects of self versus externally imposed stimulus presentation periods on memory', *Journal of Child Psychology and Psychiatry*, 33: 399–409.

Still, G.F. (1902) 'Some abnormal psychical conditions in children', *Lancet*, 1: 1077–82.

Tannock, R. (1998) 'AD/HD: advances in cognitive, neurobiological and genetic research', *Journal of Child Psychology and Psychiatry*, 39(1): 65–99.

Tattum, D. (1984) *Disruptive Pupils in Schools and Units*. Chichester: Wiley.

Taylor, E. (1995) 'Dysfunctions of attention', in D. Cicchetti and D.J. Cohen (eds), *Developmental Psychopathology, Vol. 2. Risk, Disorder and Adaptation*. New York: Wiley. pp. 243–73.

Taylor, E. (1999) 'Developmental neuropsychopathology of attention deficit and impulsiveness', *Development and Psychopathology*, 11: 607–28.

Taylor, E., Sandberg, S., Thorley, G., and Giles, S. (1991) *The Epidemiology of Childhood Hyperactivity. Maudsley Monographs No. 33*. Oxford: Institute of Psychiatry/Oxford University Press.

Teeter, P. (1998) *Interventions for AD/HD: Treatment in Developmental Context*. New York: Guilford.

Thompson, R. (1993) *The Brain: A Neuroscience Primer*. 2nd edn. New York: Freeman.

Timimi, S. (2002) *Pathological Child Psychiatry and the Medicalization of Childhood*. Bristol: Brunner-Routledge.

Van der Meere, J. (1996) 'The role of attention', in S. Sandberg (ed.), *Monographs in Child and Adolescent Psychiatry: Hyperactivity Disorders of Childhood*. Cambridge: Cambridge University Press.

Vivian, L. (1994) 'The changing pupil population of schools for pupils with emotional and behavioural difficulties', *Therapeutic Care and Education*, 3(3): 218–31.

Vygotsky, L.S. (1962) *Thought and Language*. Cambridge, MA: MIT.

Vygotsky, L.S. (1987) *The Collected Works of L.S. Vygotsky* edited by R. Reiber and A. Corton. London: Plenum.

Webber, R. and Butler, T. (2006) *Classifying Pupils by Where They Live: How Well Does This Predict Variations in Their GCSE Results?* London: CASA.

Weiss, G. and Hechtman, L. (1993) *Hyperactive Children Grown Up*. 2nd edn. New York: Guilford Press.

West, M.A. and Poulton, B.C. (1997) 'Primary health care teams: rhetoric versus reality' in M.A. West and J. Slater (eds), *Teamworking in Primary Health Care: A Review of its Effectiveness*. Research Report prepared for the Health Education Authority, London.

Weyandt, L.L. and Willis, W.G. (1994) 'Executive functions in school aged children: potential efficacy of tasks in discriminating clinical group', *Developmental Neuropsychology*, 10: 27–38.

Wood, D. (1988) *How Children Think and Learn*. Oxford: Basil Blackwell.

Woods, D.R. (1994) *Problem-based Learning: How to Gain the Most from PBL*. Canada: Donald Woods.

World Health Organization (WHO) (1990) *International Classification of Diseases*, 10th edn. Geneva: WHO.

Yerbury, M. (1997) 'Issues in multidisciplinary teamwork for children with disabilities', *Child: Care, Health, and Development*, 23(1): 77–86.

Zentall, S.S. (1995) 'Modifying classroom tasks and environments', in S. Goldstein (ed.), *Understanding and Managing Children's Classroom Behaviour*. New York: John Wiley.

Zentall, S.S. and Smith, Y.N. (1992) 'Assessment and validation of the learning and behavioural style preferences of hyperactive and comparison children', *Learning and Individual Differences*, 4: 25–41.

Zentall, S.S., and Meyer, M.J. (1987) 'Self-regulation of stimulations for ADD-H children during the reading and vigilance task performance', *Journal of Abnormal Child Psychology*, 15: 519–36.

INDEX

Added to a page number 'f' denotes a figure.

accountability 57
action plan, to support child's behaviour 66–8
active learning styles 79
ADD 4, 5
ADHD
  assessment 9
  case studies *see* case studies
  changing the course of 84–5
  client-centred approach 85–6
  cognitive ability 8–9
  developmental course 2
  diagnosis 9, 51, 90
  educational challenge 39–42
  educational engagement, limited opportunities 74
  environmental influences 12
  evidence base for
    bio-psycho social construct 8
    cognitive process 6–8
  evolution into educational issue 5–6
  heterogeneity of 9
  hyperactivity 4, 82, 91
  impulsiveness 3, 5–6, 92
  inattentiveness 2-3, 5, 7
  inclusive education 30-2, 41
  individual's experience 14–15
  interventions
    educational 70–83
    effective 29
    see also medication
  numbers of children affected 2
  nurture groups 81–2
  positive qualities 68
  schooling, experience of 33–9
  social, emotional and behavioural correlates 4–5
  support
    for coping with 87–90
    perceptions of effective 45–7
    practical classroom 50–1
  symptoms 2, 4, 5, 9
American Educational Research Association 72
assessment 9, 54
attention deficit disorder *see* ADD
attention deficit hyperactivity disorder *see* ADHD
autonomy 57

beaded-methylphenidate 26
behaviour, action plan to support 66–8
behaviour management 2, 33–6
behaviour modelling 80
behavioural charts 33, 34
beliefs 8, 25
bio-psychosocial construct 8
bio-psychosocial model 63, 64f
Boxall profile 42
British Psychological Society (BPS) 57, 60
budget holding 57

care co-ordinators 55
case studies
  behavioural difficulties in home and school setting 15–20
  different perspectives and responses 10–12
  effects of seeing ADHD as a within-child problem 36–9
  medication
    different perspectives on effects of 20-4, 29
    and environment 48–50
  perceptions of effective support 45–7
childcare, macro approach to 52
children
  beliefs about ADHD 25
  involving in collaborative working 53–5
  numbers affected 2
  objectification of 34
  support for coping with ADHD 87–90
  see also pupils
Children Act (1989) 53
classroom support, practical 50–1
classrooms, properly functioning 76
client-centred approach 85–6
co-morbid disorders 5
Code of Practice (DfES) 52, 53
cognitive ability 8-9
cognitive behavioural therapy 27, 78
cognitive deficits 77, 78
cognitive distortions 77
cognitive outcomes 80–1
cognitive research 6–7
cognitive skills, higher-level 3
cognitive strategies 76–8
collaborative programmes 56

collaborative working
  evidence of 55–6
  framework for 59–60
  involving children in 53–5
  models
    bio-psychosocial 63, 64f
    example of utilizing 66–8
    Leicester model 62–3
    problem-based learning 60–2
    progressive focusing model 65
  need for 51–3
  in schools
    making it work 56–7
    suggestions of what to do 57–8
  to identify contributing factors of ADHD 85–7
  to support children to cope with ADHD 87–90
common-sense theories 72
communication strategy 35–6
community mental health teams (CMHTs) 57
Concentra 26
concentration 3
consistency, in classrooms 51
consultation, professionals, agencies and disciplines 60
continual professional development 86
craft knowledge 73
craft persons 72

decision-making
  impulsive behaviour research 3
  involvement of parents and children 53, 54
  pedagogical 73, 77
'defect of moral control' 5
delay aversion 3
diagnosis 9, 51, 90
diagnostic criteria 5, 9, 14–15, 76, 91–2
Diagnostical and Statistical Manual of Mental Disorders
        (DSM) 5, 9, 14–15
discipline 51
dopamine 7

Education Act (1993) 52
educational achievement 32
educational challenge 39–42
educational engagement 41–2, 74
educational interventions 70–83
educational strategies 78–81
effective pedagogy, teachers' knowledge of 74–5
effective teaching and learning 71–2, 74
emotional development 52
empowerment model 57
environment, and medication 48–50
environmental influences 12
Every Child Matters: Change for Children 32, 53
Excellence for All Children (DfEE) 52, 54
executive functions, problems 6, 7, 78
extrinsic rewards 2

factory model, education 76
family environment 7–8
fixing effect, medication 28–9

genetic research 7
glossary 93–4

hedonistic behaviour 6
heterogeneity, of ADHD 9
home, support within 89–90
Hyperactive Child Syndrome 5
hyperactivity 4, 82, 91
hyperkinesis 4
Hyperkinetic Reaction of Childhood 5

identical twins, ADHD in 7
impulsiveness 3, 5–6, 92
inattentiveness 2–3, 5, 7
inclusive education 30–2, 41
inclusive schools 34
Index for Inclusion 31–2
inhibitory control system 7
instructors 76
intelligence quotient 9
inter-professional education, Leicester model 62–3
interagency working 86, 90
internal dialogue 77
internalized speech 7
intervention
  effective 29
  multi-modal 81
  see also educational interventions; medication
intrinsic interest 2

knowledge
  of effective pedagogy 74–5
  professionals reluctance to share 86

learning, effective 74
Leicester model 62–3
location, of pupils 32
low self-esteem 34

mainstream schools 31, 32, 40–1
medication
  assumption of bio-medical definition 81
  case studies
    different perspectives on effects of 20–4, 29
    and environment 48–50
  effectiveness studies 27–8
  limitations of 24–5
  monitoring 52
  psycho-stimulants 26–7
  value as support for ADHD 28–9
Metadate-CD 26
methylphenidate 26–7, 51
Minimal Brain Dysfunction 5

morbid inattentiveness 5
'more enduring characteristics' 73
motivation 2, 3
motivational appraisal 7
motor activities 4
motor control 3
multi-modal approaches 28, 81
multidisciplinary working 51–3, 55, 60

National Institute for Clinical Excellence 51
National Institute of Mental Health (NIMH) 27
neurological explanations 3, 6–7
neurotransmitters 7, 27
nurture groups 81–2

objectification 34
on-task verbal participation 79, 80
'organisation of experience' 45
organization, teamwork 57
Our Healthier Nation (DOH) 52

parents
    involvement in schools 53
    management of child behaviours 86–7
    partnerships with professionals 57, 58, 87
pathologizing 68
pedagogical decision-making 73, 77
pedagogy, knowledge of effective 74–5
peer tutoring 80
performance targets 40
positive qualities 68
positive reinforcement 80
practical theorizing 75
proactive approach, behaviour management 35
problem-based learning 60–2
professional development programme 75
professionals
    consultation between 60
    partnerships with parents 57, 58, 87
    reluctance to share knowledge 86
progressive focusing model 65
psycho-stimulants
    concerns about 27
    how they work 27
    methylphenidate 26–7, 51
pupils
    how teachers think about 73
    see also children

questioning techniques 79

reactive approaches, behaviour management 35
recess deprivation 79
reconstitution of behavioural synthesis 7
reflection 75
response inhibition 7
Ritalin 26
routine (classroom) 51

scaffolding 74
school exclusion 4
schooling, experience of 33–9
schools
    ADHD 30–43
    collaborative working 56–8
    support within 88–9
self-choose 2
self-control 7
self-direction 81
self-esteem, low 34
self-instruction techniques 77–8
self-monitoring strategies 78
self-pace/pacing 2, 80, 81
self-regulation 3, 76
self-reinforcement of desired behaviours 77
settings, educational 41, 42
social construction 8
social constructivism 75
social, emotional and behavioural correlates 4–5
social inclusion 31
socioeconomic status, educational achievement 32
special education 72
special educational needs 32, 53
Special Educational Needs Code of Practice 52, 53
specialist educational provision 4, 32
staff-pupil ratios 81
support
    in the classroom 50–1
    for coping with ADHD 87–90
    perceptions of effective 45–7
    value of medication as 28–9
sustained attention hypothesis 2
symptoms 2, 4, 5, 9
systemic analysis model 65

talkativeness 79
teacher direction 80
teacher-pupil ratios 76, 80
teachers
    how they think 72–3
    as instructors 76
    knowledge of effective pedagogy 74–5
teaching, effective 71–2, 74
teaching styles 76–7
teamwork 55, 57
theorizing, practical 75
typing 73, 74

universal entitlement, to education 30–1

verbal fluency 8–9
verbal interaction 80
visual motor tasks 78–9

working memory, impairment 7
working together see collaborative working